DR. MELVYN KINDER
AND DR. CONNELL COWAN

Bestselling authors of
SMART WOMEN/FOOLISH CHOICES

HUSBANDS

AND

WIVES

THE GUIDE FOR
MEN AND WOMEN WHO
WANT TO STAY MARRIED

THE LONG-NEEDED GUIDE FOR MEN AND WOMEN WHO WANT TO STAY MARRIED

In this groundbreaking book, authors Cowan and Kinder show husbands and wives how they can enrich and enliven their marriage, as they discuss fully and frankly sex, money, work, infidelity, domestic strife, and all the other hurdles facing couples in marriage today:

—How to transform the marital disenchantment of the '80s into a self-directed, enduring marriage of the '90s

—How to understand the paradox of change in marriage—when demanding less can create the potential for realizing more

—How couples can create bonds of friendship they never thought possible

—How affairs actually expose what's missing within ourselves and rarely what's missing in our mates

—Why sexual disinterest is not inevitable and how couples reignite passion and desire

HUSBANDS AND WIVES

DR. MELVYN KINDER received his doctorate in clinical psychology from UCLA. In addition to his writing, lectures, and workshops, he is co-director of the Westridge Psychiatric Medical Group and in private practice in Los Angeles.

DR. CONNELL COWAN received his doctorate in clinical psychology from the University of Houston. In addition to writing and conducting workshops, he is in private practice in Los Angeles.

HUSBANDS AND WIVES

Exploding Marital Myths
Deepening Love and Desire

by
Dr. Melvyn Kinder
and
Dr. Connell Cowan

A SIGNET BOOK

SIGNET
Published by the Penguin Group
Penguin Books USA Inc., 375 Hudson Street,
New York, New York 10014, U.S.A.
Penguin Books Ltd, 27 Wrights Lane,
London W8 5TZ, England
Penguin Books Australia Ltd, Ringwood,
Victoria, Australia
Penguin Books Canada Ltd, 2801 John Street,
Markham, Ontario, Canada L3R 1B4
Penguin Books (N.Z.) Ltd, 182–190 Wairau Road,
Auckland 10, New Zealand

Penguin Books Ltd, Registered Offices: Harmondsworth, Middlesex, England

This edition published by arrangement with Clarkson N. Potter, Inc.

First Signet Printing, May, 1990
10 9 8 7 6 5 4 3 2 1

PUBLISHER'S NOTE
This is a work of fiction. Names, characters, places, and incidents either are
the product of the author's imagination or are used fictitiously, and any
resemblance to actual persons, living or dead, events, or locales is entirely
coincidental.

*To my wife, Sara, who helped me recognize
the many faces of love and acceptance.*
M. K.

*To my wife, Casey, for your undaunted willingness
to engage in the never-ending adventure of marriage.*
C. C.

Acknowledgments

We wish to express our warm appreciation to Joan Stewart, our literary agent, for her unswerving belief in us and for her thoughtful encouragement and feedback throughout the preparation of the book.

Special thanks to Carol Southern for her generous and energetic efforts in guiding the work to its completion. Our thanks also to Amy Schuler for her editorial assistance and to Elaine Koster and the editorial staff of NAL for their constructive and cogent reactions to the work. And finally, we wish to extend our thanks to Barbara Marks, who has worked so hard in mapping the strategy for bringing this book to the attention of its readers.

Contents

CHAPTER ONE

The Clash
of Expectations

*W*hen we marry, we feel a delightful sense of unity with our partner. Even though we are aware of personal differences, they seem insignificant in those wonderfully accepting early stages of marriage. It's not that we don't know the odds, but we are sure we will beat them. It isn't that we naively think our marriage will be free from conflict and disappointment, but we believe our love is strong enough to conquer such obstacles and retain its passion and vitality.

But, as experience continually proves, heartfelt promises and vows alone can't forge a lasting bond between a wife and husband. This is why millions of couples secretly sense that their marriage is failing or falling far short of expectations. They feel disillusioned rather than hopeful, and they don't know how to renew the initial bright promise of marriage.

This book explores myths about love and marriage that can lead to such disenchantment, and to blame, guilt, resentment, and a pervasive pessimism.

In our previous books, *Smart Women/Foolish Choices* and *Women Men Love/Women Men Leave*, we tried to strip away the layers of foolish and unrealistic expectations that impeded both men and women in the search for a committed relationship. This book has a similar intent. In our psychotherapy practices and our work in marriage counseling, we have found that emotional impasses can be overcome only when both parties understand the foolishly unrealistic expectations—often unconscious—that they bring to marriage.

It is not enough, however, for couples merely to learn another list of dos and don'ts. This book is not intended to be a marriage manual or a "cookbook" providing simple surefire recipes for enlivening a relationship. In our experience, those approaches never work. Instead, we believe the key to making marriage survive is understanding and accepting one's mate the way that person *really* is. In this book, we hope to show couples how to erase the myths that obstruct that vision.

THE RISE OF THE OTHER-DIRECTED MARRIAGE

In the 1960s, men and women began to explore a new way of looking at life—of considering their dreams, options, and individual potential. This period has consequently been called the "me generation" or "era of narcissism." It was characterized by an emphasis on feelings rather than thinking and rationality. Openness, communication, and the expression of honest emotions were valued, even cherished, as the essential prerequisites for developing authentic bonds of intimacy.

While this period certainly broke new ground in some daring and exciting ways, it also sowed the seeds for the discontent and disenchantment that many couples suffer today.

In the 1970s, traditional marriage came under siege. It was viewed as overly restrictive to personal growth, oppressive to women especially, and in need of a major overhaul. Marriage was no longer seen as a cooperative and collaborative venture; it became merely another vehicle for personal gratification. People began to ask themselves "What am I *getting out of* the marriage?" rather than "What do I *bring to* the marriage?" The notion of "for better or worse" or "till death do us part" gave way to "till you no longer meet my needs." No wonder, then, that the divorce rate skyrocketed during the 1970s.

Thus began the Other-Directed marriage—a union in which each partner secretly holds the other responsible for happiness and fulfillment. This was a relationship based more on demanding rather than on giving.

But ironically, the Other-Directed marriage failed to provide the very rewards it seemed to promise. Expression of needs became the prelude to blame and disappointment.

Flawed as it was, the Other-Directed marriage might have survived had several social upheavals not pushed many relationships to the breaking point. The women's movement shook up traditional roles and responsibilities, demanding dramatic redefinitions. The influx of wives into the workplace forever changed the division of labor and the emotional tone in millions of homes. Marriage had to change, but much too often it didn't.

And today, in the 1980s, couples are still struggling to overcome long-venerated beliefs and mythologies that simply don't serve contemporary realities.

THE ROOTS
OF DISENCHANTMENT

Soon after we marry, reality rudely begins to intrude upon fantasy. This time is the so-called "period of adjustment." As we become more familiar with our partner on a day-to-day basis, imperfections become glaring. Minor annoyances loom large, and even freely given romantic gestures now seem stingily meted out.

Perhaps the most significant change in our thinking during this phase is the painful realization that certain expectations will not be met, and perhaps not even acknowledged as valid by our mate. Gradually, reality replaces ideal-ized and romanticized images. We begin to fight; we can't agree or compromise. We defend the boundaries of our two separate identities, and so the fantasy of oneness erodes.

But naturally, the fault lies with our mate. Surely it's the other person who has changed. Our mate has let us down. It's not that *we* have expected or assumed too much. *We* are the in-nocent victim. Or are we? Perhaps we have placed the responsibility for a successful mar-riage too far outside of ourselves.

In every marriage there exist two unwritten "contracts." The first marital contract is the one with which we are most familiar. It is the set of traditional guidelines we work out with our mate over a period of time, providing answers to such questions as how we feel about infidelity, whether we will have children, where we will live, who will work and who does what tasks, and so on.

While the first marriage contract is usually freely discussed, the second generally remains secret, implicit, and largely unconscious. It is negotiated privately by men and women in their own minds. The second contract specifies stan-dards and behaviors our partner will be ex-pected to fulfill. This second marriage contract has as its chief hallmark the secret belief that our own feelings, needs, and sense of what is right are most important.

For example, a wife may expect her husband to make her life whole, meaningful, and complete. A husband may want a wife who "does it all"—as an exemplary homemaker, mother, and sex goddess. These demands may be exhausting. The husband whose wife pleads with him to be more "open" is puzzled and confused that actions and intentions don't speak for themselves. The wife who merely wants more closeness and emotional intimacy gets upset when her husband accuses her of an insatiable demand for romantic intensity.

As this clash in expectations grows, many couples try to talk themselves through their problems. Unfortunately, such conversations are rarely objective or fruitful. This is because we rarely ask if our own expectations are fair and reasonable—we just complain endlessly. And the result is that our partner feels more guilty and inadequate.

HUSBANDS AND WIVES: AN EMOTIONAL IMPASSE?

The notion of a "battle of the sexes" has been around for so long we can now accept it as truth, and perhaps even as an intriguing and essential element in the mystery of attraction. Men and women are different, and these very differences spark love, romance, and sexual desire. However, disparate attitudes may also threaten the partnership of marriage.

Whenever marital conflicts are discussed, many

people take it for granted that husbands and wives have common wishes, concerns, and difficulties. There is an almost automatic assumption that we're all in the same boat. In the past, this may have been closer to the truth. But today, something is happening—men and women have widely divergent attitudes about marriage and their spouses, and these feelings have created a kind of emotional impasse in many marriages.

The marriage of the late 1980s is very different from marriage in preceding generations. Social changes have influenced husbands and wives in strikingly different ways. Curiously, the net effect of all these changes is that our expectations are greater than ever, while our hopes for fulfillment are smaller than ever.

What Wives Feel Today

For many American women, marriage appears to be a mixed blessing. They feel disappointed, frustrated, and powerless—unable to create the warm and fulfilling relationship they desire. They see their husbands as concerned primarily with working or finding escapist outlets, and as unresponsive to their wives' emotional needs.

Stephanie is 32 and married for the second time five years ago. A legal secretary, she reluctantly sends her two young children to a daycare center each day. "It's not what I hoped it would be," says Stephanie, shaking her head. "I work every bit as hard as Charlie and still feel responsible for most of the housework. He does wash the dishes—a bit self-righteously, I might add—and he's great with the kids, but I feel shut out. We rarely talk anymore about anything personal, or just about us as a couple. What's most maddening is that he doesn't see that anything is wrong, or at least he doesn't own up to it. I still love him, but I don't know what to do about it."

Polly, 47, has quite a good marriage, although she often questions it. Married now for almost twenty years, Polly says, "I've learned to pay less attention to the things that irritate me and more attention to those things I like about Bill. But sometimes—when I read articles about those things you should expect in a relationship, or when one of my single friends points out something I shouldn't put up with in Bill—I mistrust myself. I wonder if I'm settling for too little or should expect something more or better."

Both of these women want to be happy, want to value and enjoy marriage, and neither plans to leave. And yet each feels unsettled, vaguely dissatisfied. Why? Are these women too demanding, or are the men they love worse than they think? Probably neither is true. We have treated many such women, and we believe the seeds of their disappointment grow out of heightened and unrealistic expectations. Add to that an Other-Directed attitude—a belief that marital satisfaction is something you get your spouse to do for you—and you have all the necessary ingredients for an emotional clash or impasse.

What Husbands Feel Today

Married men today seem peculiarly complacent. One would think they would be more unsettled than they are, given all the attempts on the part of women to urge and even demand that they become more responsive than they now are. Indeed, one would expect husbands to be as frustrated as wives. If anything, however, husbands today seem quite satisfied.

The dictionary defines *complacency* as a feeling of self-satisfaction and contentment. But the word also means being unaware of danger. We believe both these definitions apply to the complacency of a great number of husbands today. They are actually much more satisfied than their wives would care to acknowledge, and too oblivious to some substantial, unresolved marriage dilemmas.

While it may be surprising to many wives today, there are scores of truly satisfied husbands. Many of them have gone through a genuine evolution in how they view themselves as men and husbands. When the women's movement first created ripples, and then waves, in the relations between the sexes, men came under attack and felt misunderstood, and at times even wrongly accused. For some, beneath their complacency there may be anger and irritation which is contained, and expressed only in a passive-aggressive and therefore manipulative and indirect fashion.

There *are* many husbands today who are content with their marriages. Alex, 35, laughingly notes how women and men seem to have reversed roles. "I love being married, coming home every night, eating a good dinner, sitting with my wife in front of the TV and just relaxing. I don't even have any desire to go out with the guys at night. It's my wife who's always talking about going out more, doing things. If we fight about anything, it's that." Alex is a husband who reflects a new kind of man today—longing for a refuge from the hassles of work, and very content in a secure and monogamous relationship.

However, some men merely appear complacent. Their wives more accurately characterize them as insensitive and indifferent. Jerry, 42, says, "Things are okay until my wife starts complaining about one thing or another. I try to humor her out of it. She never seems satisfied with our relationship. She accuses me of not communicating and being too wrapped up in work. Every now and then she trots out the same old suggestion about seeing a marriage counselor, and I tell her we can solve our own problems and that things are okay anyway." Jerry is only superficially indifferent. In a passive-aggressive fashion, he covers up his resentment of her criticisms by trivializing her concern.

Still other husbands appear complacent but feel an emotional hunger and restlessness similar to the feelings experienced by their wives. Mitchell, 41, says, "My wife used to be my best friend, but over the years we've slowly drifted apart. We don't laugh the way we used to. We barely make love anymore except now and again, so we don't have to acknowledge how unromantic this marriage has become. I feel like I'm emotionally starved, but I don't know how to change this. I'm starting to fantasize about other women, and that scares me." Mitchell is a crisis waiting to happen. Within a very short time, someone or some event could catapult him into an affair.

Often, complacency is simply a way of ignoring or shutting out a wife's complaints. "She doesn't know what she wants anymore. And you know what? I don't care, and I don't want to have to deal with it. I'm tired of trying to be this way or that way. Nothing works anyway—so I'm just going to stop worrying about it." This is the kind of comment we are hearing more and more from husbands. Such statements echo Freud's "What do women want?"

And finally, an increasing number of husbands still believe women's fantasies are charged with a desire for the powerful, romantic, and exciting male who will provide magic and passion. However, most men don't feel they can fulfill this image, and they're tired of feeling vaguely inadequate and guilty.

We observe wives and husbands trying to figure out what is going on in marriage today. There is so much flux in marriage that no clear picture emerges, save that of men and women wanting to stay married but still feeling vaguely disappointed.

However, couples today are taking a sharp

turn back toward traditional values. Unfortunately, such attitudes have not yet been translated into behavior. Husbands and wives have not yet figured out how to harness hope to specific skills that will enrich their marriage. Nevertheless, men and women appear to sense more than ever before that the more selfish or Other-Directed ways of the past do not bring happiness—instead they invariably create frustration and loneliness.

WHY LOVE BECOMES DORMANT

The plaintive declarations are common enough—"I fell out of love," or "I just don't feel anything anymore," or "Maybe we just got tired of each other," or "Once the magic is gone, there's just no way to get it back." Because of the Other-Directed attitudes in marriage, love often becomes dormant—not dead, but painfully quiet and inactive. The process is often gradual and insidious. Often couples know this is happening to them only when they look back and reminisce about feelings of joy and aliveness, passion and eroticism, caring and tenderness—feelings which all seem faint memories.

One truth about how memory works is that painful experiences stamp themselves into consciousness more indelibly than positive ones. In some ways, this enables us to survive. It is simply more adaptive to be alert to danger and threats to our welfare. This also happens in relationships. When we have been hurt, the memory of that event is terribly vivid and lasting. Yes, it is true that at times we will suppress the pain just as children repress painful encounters with their parents, but typically we remember the event even when we wish we didn't.

Hurts and disappointments in marriage are remembered with sufficient clarity to cause us to withdraw a bit, to become insulated against further harm. It is this insulation that slowly seals off feelings of love from our spouse.

To a certain extent, we feel victimized, for we interpret our mate's insensitive conduct as thoughtless and intentional. We forget that what our mate may do that may be hurtful to us is often only our mate's way of protecting himself or herself. In therapy with a couple we often ask each of them to try looking at the other's behavior as self-protective rather than taking each action personally and assuming it is hostile. This new perspective begins an important process of understanding and acceptance, a way of reminding oneself that marriage must include notions of "for better or worse" and tolerance of differences.

For many couples, disenchantment remains a well-disguised secret, operating in a subterranean fashion. On the surface, the marriage goes on—there are good times, bad times. The disappointment husbands and wives may feel is expressed in moments of anger, resentment, and repetitive complaints about the same tired issues. For others, there is a kind of giving up, a resignation that is reflected in sadness, even depression.

Yet, for most couples, beneath the layers of accumulated hurts, the original love lies dormant but not dead. The road back to the renewal of love involves the removal of negative expectations and a subsequent emotional release. It is this release that reawakens dormant love. We believe that for the vast majority of couples, the task is not too difficult for them to take on. When the enormous rewards are sensed, husbands and wives are capable of moving beyond the bad times and reconnecting with each other in new and fulfilling ways.

WHY MARRIAGE COUNSELING SO OFTEN FAILS

Unrealistic expectations create tension and frustration in marriage, and then husbands and wives make matters worse by attempting to negotiate their needs. Because we have all been so programmed to look outside of ourselves for answers, to be Other-Directed rather than Self-Directed, we have been led to think that everything that bothers us should be negotiated. We have somehow come to believe that the marriage vows have mysteriously been amended to "Love, honor, cherish, and negotiate."

Whenever a couple comes into marriage counseling, they typically ask, "What can we do to fix things?" That is their first mistake, and unfortunately it is usually compounded by the counselor, who then is spurred into some premature actions designed to provide magical answers and a variety of marital "exercises." Many couples who divorce had first sought marriage counseling, which obviously failed.

For most marriage counselors and therapists, the standard prescription for solving marital tensions is "better communication," which, of course, is simply a prerequisite for negotiation. But in our experience, a couple's talking endlessly about their needs only compounds the problem. They all too often grow increasingly frustrated, saying, "I give up—we've tried everything." Most communication in marriage today has little to do with exchanging new information and everything to do with blaming and complaining. The net effect is even more disappointment. Communication has been grossly overvalued.

But if communication and negotiation are not the answers, then what is? Is there some other way to resolve conflict and revive the marriage promise?

We believe there is. In our work with couples, we have found there are very specific actions husbands and wives can take that reverse the process of disenchantment and lead to a renewal of love. Instead of creating a courtroom atmosphere filled with marital accusations, plea bargaining, and negotiations, we have evolved a new way of dealing with marriage. We instruct wives and husbands how to begin perceiving and thinking differently about marriage in general and their own relationship in particular.

Our solution is based on an understanding of the marriage system and a model of change that is radically different from that which people are traditionally taught. Much of it emphasizes that what you *do* has a much greater impact that what you *say*. Actions have always spoken louder than words—in marriage especially. Somehow, many people have forgotten that. Our approach focuses on helping husbands and wives to become Self-Directed, showing them what each of them can do themselves to enhance the quality of the marriage experience rather than reinforcing futile attempts to get the other person to change.

BECOMING SELF-DIRECTED

First, each of us must identify and recognize the inaccurate and exaggerated expectations we hold and then take responsibility for them. By doing this we can learn to gradually remove these expectations from the marriage system and thereby create room for change. In doing this, we release both ourselves and our mates from being accountable for both the joys and the disappointments in our marriages. Learning how to take greater charge of our own fulfillment by standing back and doing what we can do on our own creates an emotional release—we "let go" of our negative attachment to our mate. When this is accomplished, the atmosphere changes, and the other person has to respond in a different way. For example, when someone doesn't feel criticized, he or she is much more likely to give freely.

The implications of this new approach are enormous. It takes two people to have a marriage, but only one to change it. We end up feeling helpless and out of control in our marriages simply because we can't control our partners. The truth is that we need only learn to control ourselves. We ultimately come to feel alone in our marriages because we have replaced an accepting attitude toward our partner with unconscious expectations that are ultimately self-defeating.

Being Self-Directed empowers husbands and wives. Rather than feeling victimized and ineffective, they can regain greater control over their own lives and marital experiences. As they willingly abandon attempts to change their mates and instead focus on themselves, changes surprisingly and predictably occur in their marriages. As psychologists, we know that if you change yourself, the system changes, and finally your mate will invariably respond to the change. We recognize that in most marriages, one partner may be more reluctant or less motivated to take on the work involved in changing a marriage. But using our approach, an individual can effect powerful changes with or without his or her mate's direct participation!

Our purpose is to help couples find solutions to the disappointment they feel and to equip a husband or wife with attitudes and strategies that create change even if he or she is the only one working on the relationship.

We are hopeful and optimistic about the future of marriage. We believe that most couples are committed to marriage in spite of their present frustrations. As we've said, even good marriages have bad times. But when couples understand the reasons why marriages evolve in the way they do, they can begin to overcome these predictable dilemmas. When they shift from "demanding" thinking to "accepting" thinking, they end up not settling for less, but ultimately getting much more and making their marriage come alive again.

CHAPTER TWO

Letting Go of Marital Myths

*W*e all have a system of beliefs within us that is composed of what we know, or think we know, about men, women, and relationships. These beliefs and assumptions typically operate on a reflexive and unconscious level and shape how we behave, what we expect, and how we feel about the direction our life is taking. We are supposedly more sophisticated about love and marriage than previous generations were. We are subjected to articles, books, and television programs whose purpose it is to illuminate the pitfalls and promises of love. We hear surveys that, depending on the current trend, either paint a rosy picture of love or, as is more often the case, portray frustration, alienation, and disillusionment. There are grains of truth in what we see and hear, but there are also misunderstandings, distortions, and myths, especially about the nature of marriage.

Most of us learn about marriage firsthand through an often frustrating, sometimes painful process of trial and error, occasionally hurting ourselves and our mates. We haven't been taught in any systematic fashion what we might expect or what might be expected of us. Instead, we pick up bits and pieces of information along the way from parents, early romantic adventures, and the media—some of it accurate and helpful but unfortunately much of it inaccurate and distorted.

Because of the rise of the Other-Directed marriage, virtually every couple have particular beliefs that are harmful to the life of the relationship. We are going to describe some of these myths—erroneous beliefs and assumptions about marriage that lead to expectations that are at best unrealistic, and at worst foolish and destructive. When we examine marriages close up and attempt to understand dissatisfactions and tensions, we find that couples are not necessarily incompatible, but their expectations are.

While anyone who is observant about marriage today knows there is a clash of expectations that creates frustration and disappointment, it is our belief that husbands and wives inadvertently create many of these tensions themselves. It is not necessarily one's mate who is the problem. More often than not, the very heart of the difficulty may lie within yourself and what you believe to be true about marriage in general. In working with couples, we often hear some variation of "Isn't it reasonable for him to do this?" or "All I want is for her to act fairly." It is when "reasonable" expectations seem to be thwarted or ignored that disillusionment and frustration result. Even more difficult are those expectations that are implicit rather than conscious, that are always assumed to be part of any "good" marriage.

As you read about these myths, be alert to the ways in which they crop up in your own thinking and in your communications with your spouse. Recognizing the existence of these self-defeating beliefs is possible for anyone who knows where to look and who has the courage to peel away the distorted half-truths about marriage. This is the first step toward becoming Self-Directed in your marriage and able to effect changes in your relationship.

Be very careful not to misinterpret our basic message. We believe marriage can provide wondrous returns on anyone's emotional investment. There is a specialness about the marital bond that sets it above just about any other relationship. So we are not asking you to "settle" or telling you that your dreams of what a husband or wife can provide are unattainable. But we are saying that it is critical to examine some of the wishes and expectations you bring to marriage, understand their origins, and then approach your mate with a sense of the possible rather than the impossible.

You will notice that some of these myths are

old and traditional in the sense that couples
have always believed them to be true and they
have always created dissension in marriage. A
number of the other myths, however, are new,
unfortunate by-products of the "me generation"
and the excessive psychologizing of marriage to
the point where anything seems possible and
reasonable if only you just talk about it and
negotiate it long enough.

Myth #1
Marriage will make you feel
complete and whole.

This is the most widely held myth in marriage.
No matter how emotionally healthy or how in-
telligent we are, most of us harbor the secret
and largely unconscious fantasy that marriage
will make us feel safe, whole, and complete in a
way that being single can never do.

As we develop from infancy to adulthood,
we must learn to separate from our parents and
evolve our own distinct and unique identity.
Most of us complete this process successfully,
and yet there is always some sense of loneliness
or lack of completion. As adults, we often yearn
for that primitive sense of oneness we felt as
infants—that feeling of total safety and security
we had before any dawning awareness that life
is a solo experience, begun, lived, and ended
fundamentally alone.

When we search for a life mate, a common

secret wish is that together we will be as one. This is the fuel that drives romance and secret longings—the fantasy of fusion. We feel we have a hedge against loneliness and isolation when we are together, and, conversely, when our lover or mate is not with us, we may feel fragmented, less than a whole person. The truth is that as social beings, we all have a hunger for love and human contact—and marriage may go a long way toward satisfying this hunger. However, it cannot satisfy our most primitive longings and fantasies about completion. The expectation that it will is inevitably frustrated. Feelings of warmth, safety, and wholeness—of complete union—can only be attained in a system without conflict or differences. The very moment differences arise, these feelings are threatened—if we don't feel especially close, we feel especially far away. Marriage is a system that has built-in differences. Wives and husbands who insist they could be as one with their mate if only their mate did this or that are playing out a belief in this myth.

The implicit belief that marriage should make us feel whole leads to a wide range of marital conflicts. If we feel insecure or depressed, for example, we may automatically look to our spouse as the antidote to these negative feelings. Either we want our mate to solve the problem, or we secretly blame him or her for somehow not being enough for us—not loving enough, not rich enough, not sexual enough, not "something" enough.

"I always felt we should do everything together," Maggie says with a shake of her head. "I figured when you're married and really love each other, then you want to do things together. Well, I got a real dose of reality recently. We happened to be taking a long weekend with some people my husband and I had only met recently. Daniel had to leave to take care of some business, which meant I'd be alone with these people for a day and an evening. I made a big fuss and made him feel guilty about leaving. The truth is that I was feeling uncomfortable about being on my own with our new friends. I suddenly realized how much I'd come to depend upon his taking the lead in social situations and protecting me from ever really dealing with my shyness. Even though I kept telling myself I wanted to be with him because it was the 'loving' thing to do, I knew deep inside I was avoiding being alone with people I didn't know really well. I guess that doesn't have as much to do with love as it does with feeling incomplete or being afraid I'm not interesting enough when I'm by myself and not part of a couple."

Maggie has learned a valuable lesson: marriage is not a solution to problems with confidence and self-esteem. It wasn't until she found the courage to honestly face her personal discomfort that things began to change. "Looking back," Maggie continues, "I realize I wanted Daniel to take care of a problem I needed to deal with myself. It sounds naive now, but I had convinced myself that togetherness was what love and marriage was all about."

Marriage is ultimately about two relatively whole individuals coming together to create a union that can be even greater than the sum of the parts. But each of us must always be aware that a lack of self-confidence is our own separate job to fix. We can look to our mate for support, but not for magical solutions.

Myth #2
Your mate should change for you if he or she really loves you.

As we have noted, in recent years many couples have erroneously assumed that negotiation is a natural and basic part of marriage, that it's important to ask for what you want and need in a relationship. It is common for marriage counselors to start out the first session with a couple by saying to each party, "Tell your spouse what you need from your marriage." This approach implies that change is a result of communication. While communicating your needs may be reasonable as a starting point, it doesn't mean that what you want is something your mate can provide. Yet somehow we have been brainwashed into thinking that change, even a monumental modification of the marital bond, is entirely possible. The underlying assumption is that if your mate truly loves you, he or she will make herculean efforts to twist himself or herself into the exact shape you desire.

"I'd always thought of myself as being pretty neat," Josh says, "but neatness took on a whole new definition after Becky and I got married. At first I tried to keep up with her, but I found I couldn't. No sooner would I put a cigarette out than the ashtray would disappear for cleaning. After dinner I'd say, 'There's a great program I'd like to watch with you—I'll do the dishes afterward.' But no! She'd be in there doing the dishes while I watched the show, feeling guilty. It wasn't that she particularly enjoyed doing dishes, it was just that she couldn't stand knowing they were dirty and sitting there. We used to have these big fights where I'd tell her how compulsive she was and that I was fed up with how guilty she made me feel all the time. I've stopped doing that now. I keep my life as organized and uncluttered as I need and I don't worry that it doesn't match her level of tidiness."

Josh was smart to stop trying to change Becky. She felt vaguely anxious and out of control when her environment was in a state of disarray. In many ways, she disliked her compelling need for organization even more than Josh did; it was exhausting and time-consuming. But like it or not, neatness was a basic and persistent part of her personality style and intimately tied to her being able to feel relaxed and comfortable. Josh's acceptance of that allows them both to feel less guilty and more at ease.

Men and women have been led to believe

that change or growth is easier than it really is. The human potential movement urged men and women to change themselves, to actualize themselves, to grow and to evolve. And it apparently followed in the minds of many that if individual growth is good, so too is growth in marriage, and therefore asking a mate to change is good on two counts: it helps the marriage to change positively and it increases the chances of getting what one needs.

What is conspicuously missing in all this new thinking is the old concept of "for better or worse"—of accepting a mate's flaws as well as enjoying his or her virtues. Acceptance does not mean you have to live with conditions in your marriage that you find irritating or even intolerable. But acceptance does mean that your mate must feel confident that you love him or her in spite of any flaws, and that you can distinguish good points from imperfections.

Couples sometimes go on trying to change each other long after it is clear that it won't work. What happens is that the one who wants change begins to build a case that gets increasingly extreme and dramatic, even obsessional, as though the validity of the marriage hinged on some specific change. Getting a spouse to change becomes tantamount to getting him or her to love you.

You are allowing yourself to be influenced by this myth—equating change with love—whenever you find yourself being unrelenting in your effort to persuade your spouse to be different.

Some of the clues are constant criticism, nagging, and at times uncontrolled irritability when your mate's awful and unwanted behavior manifests itself. Again, love is about acceptance. Your mate can love you and still find it nearly impossible to modify his or her behavior in any lasting and consistent way.

No one sets out to annoy or disappoint his or her mate. We all want to please—we all want to feel our mate thinks we are terrific. But we all fall short and do things that jar, hurt, and let down our mate. Disappointment is upsetting not only to the one who feels it but also to the one who causes it. As one man revealed with great sadness, "My wife tells me she feels lonely with me sometimes because I don't talk about my feelings very well. It makes me feel awful and somehow defective. The truth is I guess I don't really know how to express my feelings— it's not that I don't have them, I just can't seem to let them out. I can remember as a kid being more emotional and my father calling me a 'big goddam baby.' It was easier keeping my mouth shut."

A spouse may want to change but somehow find it painfully difficult to do so. Many of our personality traits were developed as a means to protect ourselves from psychological harm. Today, we may not need these defense mechanisms, but nevertheless they persist. As much as we may want to modify them, unconsciously we still feel we need them. Those traits you find annoying or maddening are, for the other person, ways of coping and surviving that are very difficult to shed.

The ease or difficulty of responding to your mate's request for change is often totally independent of how much you love your mate. As psychotherapists, we struggle every day trying to help people let go of old behaviors and find the courage to risk new ones. All of these people want to change, and for the most part they love their spouses.

Myth #3
If you truly love each other, romance should continue to flourish.

Romantic feelings and love are linked yet vastly different psychological states of mind. Romance is characterized by feelings of rare closeness, ecstasy, longing, and idealization. We feel that we and our mate are as one, soulmates. In the beginning stages of any relationship we all look for that exquisite feeling of excitement and infatuation, that heightened sense of aliveness.

But no matter how wonderful we feel, there is still a basic truth lurking in the background: romance is based more on fantasy than on reality. Romance is more about what we project into the situation than about what is actually there. It is based on mystery, fantasy, hopes, and wishes. Our lover's flaws are minimized and his or her virtues are magnified in our eyes. So, as we come to know more about our lover, romance evolves into something more real and substantial, though often less intoxicating. Love, based upon information and experience, takes over where romance leaves off.

While romance often leads to love and marriage, it doesn't automatically follow that love leads to romance. When a man and a woman love each other, the way in which that love is expressed is quite varied. Love is about loyalty, fidelity, and companionship. It is about shared dreams, tenderness, and sexuality. For some couples, an ongoing passion and excitement may also be part of the story. But for others, romance and passion become rare and fleeting experiences in the marriage. In other words, romantic interludes need not be absent from the marriage, but they are not automatic simply because two people love each other.

We do not intend just to offer a sobering message here. There is room in any marriage for romantic moments, gestures, and experiences. Many marriages have woven into their fabric the notion of romance, and this can be true even for couples married many years. In Chapter 7 we will describe the ways in which romance can be stimulated anew and made a more permanent part of marriage.

Myth #4
Your mate should understand you.

There is one assumption about love that leads to more difficulty in marriage than almost any other, and that is the notion that when someone loves you, he or she will almost intuitively understand you. Remember how in the romantic phase of your relationship each of you sensed what the other was thinking and feeling? Some couples will say, "We know each other so well we can finish each other's sentences!" There was that feeling of being in tune that felt so wonderful. So, why shouldn't that continue on into marriage? Well, for one reason, as you relax and become accustomed to each other, part of what is so wonderful is that you don't have to attend to each other all the time; there is some lessening of the intensity of the involvement. And with that lessening of being "into" each other comes a more normal state of understanding that is dependent less on intuition and more on directly expressed information.

But as time goes on in a marriage, the partners are often saddened by the decrease in sensitivity and empathy. Couples in therapy frequently accuse each other of expecting the mate to be a "mind reader." "You should have known that would hurt me," they insist. "You knew what you were getting when we got married." "I haven't changed at all—why don't you understand me?" Such remarks tell us as therapists that spouses are assuming that a mate should have a vivid sense of who they are, what they need, what hurts them, and what makes them happy. Unfortunately, that's just not so.

How many things do you assume your mate knows about you in an active way? As the years go by, most of us have a growing list of feelings, needs, and concerns that we've long ago stopped putting into words, believing that they are obvious to our mate. It can be helpful and informative to sit down periodically and actually write out such a list and then talk about it with your partner. Often those aspects about ourselves with which we are so intimately familiar fade from our mate's consciousness if we don't occasionally put them into words. One couple, in doing this simple exercise, discovered something very interesting. The man had on his list "I assume Linda knows I love her." Linda was pleasantly surprised. "It's been a long time since he's told me he loved me," she said, to which he countered, "I guess I just thought you knew it, since I've been faithful, we have a pretty good sex life, and I keep coming home to you year after year." He believed his actions expressed his love for her. What he didn't realize is that at times we all need to hear words of reassurance to allay our normal doubts and insecurities.

Understanding is a result not only of communication but of a kind of sensitivity and heightened wish to listen well and observe with perceptiveness. But we seldom have that kind of vigilance and observational skill. Often spouses are preoccupied with their own separate concerns and apprehensions. No matter how much love we may feel for the other, there are so many feelings and wishes that we miss. The wife who is preoccupied with children and juggling her own career may not be so quick to sense her husband has had a tough day, and that is normal. The husband who comes home and greets his wife who has been talking to the schoolteacher about their child's performance may not want to pick up her cues to talk, and instead he turns on the television to watch the news. Are they selfish? Unloving? No, just human.

How many times have you said, or heard, "That's not what I meant," countered by "Well, that's what you said," countered again by "No I didn't—are you trying to tell me I'm a liar?" countered by "What are you telling me, that I'm deaf?" and so on. What do we have here, liars and deaf people? Not at all. How we act, what we say, and what we project are not necessarily what our mate receives. We are often rather blind to the exact ways in which we come across. What we feel, how we act, even what we say are so often filtered, guarded, or oblique that our mate may have a hard time trying to decipher and be understanding even if he or she is willing to make the necessary effort. The wife who expresses a wish to be heard may be perceived as a complainer rather than as someone who simply wants to be understood more clearly. The husband who wants more support for his financial concerns may be seen as tight and argumentative rather than as someone who is reaching out for help and support.

One reason why mates cannot reflexively and easily understand each other, today especially, is that we are overburdened with myths about the opposite sex that further impair our listening ability. Put bluntly, we are not even sure what it is we are supposed to be listening for! So often very legitimate pleas are misinterpreted. For example, the wife who wants more time is heard as asking for more romance, and the husband who complains about the kids' behavior may really be asking for more quiet time with his wife.

Don't automatically assume anything. Help your mate to understand you, and, above all, give up on any fantasy of an all-knowing and intuitive mate. Be clear in expressing what you feel and what you need. Your mate won't necessarily respond with eagerness, but at least you will no longer be relying on clairvoyance and mind reading.

Myth #5
Differences in need should always be negotiated.

Husbands and wives often fear differences in personality styles and values; they come to believe that similarities and love are the same.

The fear of differences exists on all levels of human behavior. Prejudices, for instance, are a result of the fear of differences. It's almost as though differences are threatening just because they sometimes make us feel uncomfortable. If people are different, we're not sure they will understand or appreciate us. If they value something we don't, does it mean they do not value who we are? Of course not. Yet we often act as if it were desperately important to make our mate become more like us.

The need to negotiate is too often motivated by an unconscious fear that differences between husband and wife will result in loneliness and isolation and perhaps lead to an affair, or even divorce. For example, a husband may try desperately, though covertly, to sabotage his wife's involvement in work or a new hobby or friendship because of his fear that she will meet new people, particularly new men, and he may lose her. Does that sound extreme? Yes, but our basic and most primitive fears do drive us to extremes.

The belief that relationships should be fine-tuned by a kind of ongoing negotiation is a rather recent phenomenon. The "psychologizing" of relationships has placed great emphasis on communication, and it has been assumed that the sole purpose of communication is negotiation, and that negotiation—asking for what you want and giving up only what you have to—is always good. But negotiation is not always good.

Far too often it is motivated more by fear and distrust than by love.

"I think we like about three quarters of each other," a married woman said, "but that last quarter of each of us is engaged in an ongoing cold war. I'm trying to get him to come around to my way of thinking and he's trying to convince me that he's right. It all gets pretty exhausting when you consider that we basically like each other."

Couples who fail to accept each other's basic personalities are often caught up in a terrible endless drama of trying to change each other. Rather than love, the commodity of exchange in these scenarios is power—the fear of not having it and the wish to possess it in order to feel more effective and worthy. Negotiation is too often a mask for old unresolved anxieties or power struggles between husbands and wives.

"Every time I open a can of beer or have a second glass of wine when we're out to dinner I try to prepare myself for that look of hers," Jesse complains of his wife, "but the corker really came the other day when we walked into a small party at a friend's house and were asked if we'd like a drink. Robin said, 'Nothing for me, thank you—one alcoholic in the family is more than enough.' " Robin grew up in the tragic chaos and unpredictability of an alcoholic family structure. Her father was the drinker and her mother inevitably played out the role of the martyr. Robin vowed she would be different and never get caught up in that painful downward spiral.

In Robin's mind, anyone who drinks with any regularity is an alcoholic or at least one in the making. She is convinced Jesse is an alcoholic even though he rarely imbibes to excess and does not drink on a nightly basis. She would like him to stop drinking altogether. He finds that totally unacceptable. Recently, she countered with what she believed to be a reasonable compromise—that he would not have any alcohol at home and would restrict his drinking to parties or dinners out. Jesse's response was one of anger and frustration. "I've heard all the horror stories," he says, "but frankly I'm sick to death of her seeing me as a stand-in for her father. Sure, her childhood was awful, but I don't do any of those things. I'm not an alcoholic, and I'm not going to hide the fact that I enjoy an occasional drink just to make her feel more comfortable and in control. I'd be more than willing to talk if I felt I had a problem, but I don't know how you negotiate moderation."

Whenever we work with couples, we are continually surprised to find that different values and ways of being are often complementary: the passive person marries the energetic and dynamic one, and the less responsible individual marries a more stable and conservative one. And then they set out to change each other! The message here is simple. Try to remember why you were attracted to your mate in the first place. Remember how at one time you delighted in and treasured some of those differences that you now may find threatening or annoying. Learn to become more accepting and to appreciate the differences between you and your mate. See them as lending variety, texture, and the potential for surprise to your relationship.

Myth #6
In a good marriage the partners have identical dreams and goals.

Wrong! Partners in a good marriage have commonly shared dreams but also individual ones. The fantasy of fusion runs throughout most marriages, but rather than leading to closeness and intimacy, it causes difficulties. Every husband and wife is a separate and distinct individual, and their different personalities lead to different ways of viewing life. Invariably couples will have attitudes and ideas about where to live, how children should be raised and where they should go to school, how to save money and plan for their retirement, for instance. In each of these areas, each spouse understandably would like the other to have the same point of view. But it never happens that way. Goals and dreams are different because each husband and wife is a unique and separate person with his or her own ideas about what is worthwhile and what is not.

"We're actually a lot more alike than we are different," Corine says. "But when it comes to money, we are like night and day. We both have the same overall goal of a secure life-style, but I just think he takes it to an extreme. He'll drive around the block ten times looking for a parking space rather than pay for a parking garage, and he throws a fit when I have someone in to clean more than once a month. The fact is, we both work and make good money, and we don't have to pinch pennies. I really had to draw the line for myself the other day when he got annoyed because I took my car to the carwash—he washes his own, of course, and thinks I should too. I ended up blowing up and telling him, 'Look, I don't get on your case simply because it's in your nature to be thrifty and want to save money when you can. That's just fine, but we are different, and I don't want to feel guilty or self-indulgent every time I choose to spend money in a little different way. We're not clones and we don't always have to think the same.' "

In a good marriage, couples should respect and appreciate the differences in their dreams and goals. Ideally these differences can become the substance and text of a lively dialogue between the two people in which both feel they "win" because they are better informed. By *dialogue*, we mean an exchange of ideas, not a tension-filled negotiation. When love exists, this kind of exchange gradually evolves into a merging or growing unity of vision. But unity is never going to be perfect. There will always be divergent views and rough edges—which, we believe, actually enhance a sense of aliveness in the marriage.

Myth #7
A marriage must be stable
in order to be healthy.

We all desire a certain degree of stability in life; otherwise there would be too much uncertainty and anxiety about the unknown. One of the reasons we get married is to provide a context or structure that feels safe and secure. "I wanted to settle down" is the reason given by many for why they chose to marry. A marriage for most of us is a kind of refuge from the difficulties of living in a complex and increasingly uncertain society.

At the same time, in most marriages there is also a secret fear of stagnation and boredom that lurks just beneath the surface. We all crave a sense of aliveness and savor significant times of passion and intensity with our mate. What we have are distinctly different needs butting head on, creating a continual conflict in marriage: our need for security and stability is at odds with our wish for surprise and the unexpected. For instance, many of us desire a very sensual and erotic mate, but we have trouble reconciling this wish with our tendency to feel jealous. How can this conflict be resolved? Well, it can't be! But that's not bad news; in fact, it is the opposition of stability and passion that provides the energy driving many very successful marriages.

It's important to understand that the marriage system is dynamic rather than static, which means that there is constant movement and change. As in all systems, there is an equilibrium point that is maintained even though at any time there may appear to be an imbalance. Some wives and husbands argue a great deal, have bouts of jealousy and dissension, and yet overall they are happy with the marriage. Outsiders observing them may wonder, "How do they stay together?" or declare, "I would never tolerate such treatment." They don't understand that for many couples, a certain level of tension seems to be required and indeed becomes the catalyst for interest, passion, and excitement.

Stability may be fine for some couples, but there are others who may desire instability even though they don't recognize that desire. If you examine your own situation and you're honest with yourself, you may find that the instability in your marriage is less a fatal flaw than a by-product of the complex ways that you relate to your mate.

It is interesting to note how often we hear cynical and disparaging comments about marriage along these lines: "There aren't any really good marriages in which both people are happy, faithful, and committed." We take firm exception to this depressing statement. Marriage— settling in for a long-term relationship—is an enormous and demanding undertaking. Like life, marriage has its failures as well as its successes; it has challenges and built-in difficulties. But in spite of the emotional roller-coaster ride that marriage can be at times, it works for many individuals in basic and important ways.

Loraine describes the success of her marriage of thirty years as somewhat of a mystery. "I don't know if I could tell you exactly what has kept us together all these years. I used to think it was the kids, but they're all grown and gone and we just keep on going. We certainly haven't had an easy life and time together. But sometimes I think people who struggle together and endure the hard times are closer than those who've had it easy. To this day, neither one of us shies away from a good fight, but I don't think either one of us would have it any other way."

Don't automatically assume instability is bad. Rather than looking too closely at your marriage, ask yourself if you really want it to be different and whether if, overall, there is a kind of predictability to the instability that makes it acceptable as long as it is kept within bounds and doesn't lead to a marital crisis. And finally, be aware that desire, excitement, and passion are oftentimes delightfully chaotic. It is a myth that stability is necessarily the ideal state between husbands and wives.

Passion and the unexpected are desired by so many men and women today, yet they fail to take responsibility for the effects of those forces on their marriage. Be honest with yourself.

Understand that you may be in exactly the kind of marriage that truly fits your needs!

Myth #8
The more open you are with your mate, the more satisfying the marriage.

This is a belief that is so pervasive it is taken as gospel by the vast majority of couples in America. It would be nice if it were true, but it's not. Relationships are not so simple that mere openness, the expression of what we think and feel, will instantly produce closeness. Like so many other myths that confuse marriage today, the idea that openness is synonymous with intimacy and is therefore a prerequisite for a good marriage may have caused as much harm as good.

The "psychologizing" of marriage in the past twenty years has led many to believe that openness is a *sine qua non* of marital health. At the risk of sounding reactionary, we hold that openness may be desirable but it need not be mandatory. Some men and women are less open, and less verbally facile, than others. However, these quieter types are often no less loving. They may express their love in a variety of nonverbal ways. They make statements about their love by what they do, by the attention they pay, and by being loyal and supportive in times of need. Men and women knew ways to show love for each other long before the psychologizing of relationships took place. Many of these ways had little or nothing to do with words.

How open can one be? We are not obliged to conceal basic truths about ourselves from our mates, nor do we have the right to use those truths as weapons against our mates. There are no marriages in which openness is entirely without boundaries. There are things you don't say, however true they may be, if the predictable effect upon your mate is emotional devastation. If you do choose to drop those nuclear bombs, you had better be prepared for the consequences. Every marriage has its secrets. Only we know the darkest corners of ourselves and all of our vulnerabilities and silent fears. Only we know the emotional details of our past relationships. What we choose to communicate to our mate is filtered and edited, and this is normal.

The emphasis upon emotional expression in recent years has probably led to more confusion than clarification. When two people express all of their feelings openly toward each other they may be a little better informed but a lot more hurt, confused, and angry.

In musing about his long and successful marriage, Al says, "I'm surprised she stuck it out in the early years. I got into this thing where I thought honesty was good for its own sake and that the only way to feel free was to say anything that was on my mind. I thought Ginny always had a problem with anger, because she didn't let it out very often. I used to blow up all the time and even feel proud of myself, as if I were the healthier one. I know now that was a lot of nonsense and pretty irresponsible of me. It was just a whole lot easier to blow off steam than it was to contain some of my frustrations. Ginny was an easy target because she didn't know how to fight back and I could rationalize the whole situation away as healthy, honest communication."

Privacy is a much-neglected concept in marriage that should be dusted off and reexamined. We believe all healthy marriages allow for some degree of aloneness, time for contemplation, and ultimately coming to grips with one's separate identity. Those who have difficulty with separateness will find themselves asking for, even demanding, openness not as a precursor to intimacy but rather as an antidote to experiencing themselves as separate individuals. Further, everyone is entitled to his or her secrets provided they are not damaging to the relationship. The need for privacy should be respected rather than condemmed.

Excessive communication about personal feelings is often a disguise for something else— accusations, blame, even manipulation. When in couples therapy one spouse says to the other, "I feel such-and-such," that person should not be surprised when that openness is met with resentment, for such disclosures are so often delivered with an unspoken barb attached: "I feel such-and-such and you are to blame."

In some of the best marriages, there is a great

deal of dialogue and communication, but it's not about the relationship itself. It is not a sharing of feelings about each other or about the marriage, but about the world and life in general. Indeed, a sense of friendship and closeness often comes about from the exchange of ideas rather than feelings, which have been so overemphasized and overglorified in recent years.

Myth #9
If two people are growing individually, it will automatically enhance their marriage.

This is another one of those truisms from the last twenty years. Psychological growth or "self-actualization" was thought to be a virtue unto itself regardless of the cost. Although there is no doubt that it is better to grow than to be a person who never learns, never does anything new, never risks exposure to new stimulations and ideas, we believe that there is an implicit marriage contract that cannot be violated. There is a certain degree of latitude in every marriage, but there are also certain boundaries and limits that must be acknowledged. For example, there is a kind of tacit understanding that develops between a husband and wife as to how much time they should spend apart and how friendly each can be with members of the opposite sex. These pacts are essential to maintaining comfort and trust in marriage. In other words, there may be limits to individual growth! That is, if one is also interested in preserving the marriage.

In a good marriage, a wife and a husband are almost intuitively aware of these unspoken contracts. They realize that while too little flux and change leads to a deadening of the marriage, too much change and divergence of values and interest can create a disequilibrium that can prove fatal.

We are not suggesting that individual growth should be curtailed; instead, we are only warning couples that individual change and stretching have effects on the marriage bond. You should be aware of these effects if you truly value your relationship.

Myth #10
Sexual disinterest is inevitable in marriage.

In a low voice and with his eyes averted, Craig told us that he and his wife of nine years had sexual contact every three or four months. "Whether we need it or not," he added sardonically. "She's sick, my back hurts, she's got her period, we're both stressed out, or we go to bed at different times—it's all those things. I'm always telling myself, 'We'll do it tomorrow,' but secretly I know that tomorrow there will be some other reason to put it off. I guess the truth is that I've just lost interest."

Craig was trying to convince himself that his waning interest was a natural and normal by-product of the passage of time. He was wrong. Naturally, the wildly exciting and exhilarating times when you can't take your hands off each other are less frequent. But passion doesn't simply die, it is systematically killed.

Before marriage, we like someone to whom we are attracted, while after marriage we are attracted to our mate because we like and are comfortable with him or her. "Liking" always gets more complicated with time. There are increasing opportunities for hurt, misunderstanding, and disappointment—the three principal diminishers of "liking." In the context of a marriage, sexual interest is intimately linked to "liking" and sexual disinterest invariably tied to unresolved and often hidden problems in the marriage.

Sexuality has always been like a magnet—drawing in our most intimate, loving, and personal feelings. But the domain of sexuality has also served as an easy place to hide feelings, to exercise power, and to manipulate our mates. In a relationship, sexuality is also the most sensitive of barometers. During times of trouble, it is the first area to be affected and the last to return to normal after problems have been resolved.

Sexual disinterest, whether in a man or a woman, is never simply a problem in itself. Rather, it is always the tip of the iceberg—a symptom of some ongoing unresolved problem in the marriage. As Judith, a woman married for six years, explains, "As far as he's concerned, I'm just not as interested as I once was. But I know it's deeper than that and has something to do with the fact that we don't talk, or when we do, we don't really say anything. I wanted our lovemaking to be a time when we felt close, but it was always hop on, hop off, roll over, and go to sleep for him. After a while it didn't mean anything anymore. Sex felt empty and I felt alone."

Judith hasn't lost interest in sexual activity, but she's hurt and angry, and her seeming disinterest is her way of indirectly broadcasting a powerful protest to her husband.

Sexual disinterest is a danger sign and one that should not be ignored. Disinterest is what we feel when we are no longer willing to feel vulnerable, hurt, angry, or anxious. It becomes easier to be disinterested than to risk disappointment or be seen as disappointing. Disinterest is the solution when we don't know what else to do about our feelings. It is not a natural by-product of the passage of time but reflects specific personal and marital issues that are not being handled by the couples in an open and positive way.

Myth #11
If you're not feeling fulfilled, your marriage must be at fault.

When we are growing up, the burden for making our lives feel "right" is squarely on the shoulders of our parents. Then during early adulthood we become painfully aware that fulfillment is our singular responsibility. When we marry, the burden is all too often put back onto our partner, who becomes an easy scapegoat for our lack of fulfillment. Marriage becomes the primary source of validation and approval.

Personal fulfillment is always our own responsibility throughout life. Fulfillment is an attitude, a feeling, a conclusion we come to about our current state of growth and well-being. Fundamentally, fulfillment is something that only we can create and give to ourselves. It's never something that is provided by another person, however generous or well-meaning that other person may be. Fulfillment is a by-product of our actions, what we do in our lives, how we use the talents and gifts that we have been given. Fulfillment comes from knowing and trusting ourselves and using that knowledge to direct ourselves toward activities and involvements that are intellectually and emotionally pleasurable, satisfying, and meaningful. Sometimes this is incredibly difficult. For men, and increasingly for women, the emphasis on success in the workplace can become so dominant that they easily miss opportunities to become involved in activities that are not tied to economic achievement and might, in fact, bring them real fulfillment. Women have their own blind spots, frequently dwelling on incomplete aspects of their relationships rather than expending energy actively in some area of life over which they have more control.

Unfortunately, our marriage partners are the easiest targets for any kind of vague dissatisfaction we feel. Marriage was never meant to be the antidote to personal difficulties or dissatisfactions, yet for most of us it assumes that position in our lives. Even though many of us know better, we continue to blame our mates for our own problems. If we are depressed, it is their fault. If we had a bad day at the office, it is their fault. If we are spending too much money, it is their fault. If sex is lousy, it is their fault. If the marriage isn't more enjoyable, more alive, and more vibrant, that is their fault too. The truth is, it's a whole lot easier to blame somebody else for something that's not quite right than it is to look inside and realize that we are the only ones who ultimately can change our experiences. Blaming our mate never changes anything and certainly never creates a sense of fulfillment; it only alienates the one we love. And perhaps even more fundamental, blame puts us out of touch with ourselves and our ability to make choices. It is only when we look to ourselves as the catalyst for meaningful experiences that we have a chance to change our life.

Making someone else responsible for our fulfillment also leads to another predictable outcome: guilt. Since no one really can fulfill anyone else, most marriage partners feel some sense of guilt at having let down their mates. This kind of guilt unfortunately never brings us closer to our mates. Rather it drives a silent wedge between us. Moreover, guilt is always accompanied by resentment and a wish to retaliate.

When we are not feeling fulfilled, the problem is not necessarily that there is something wrong with the marriage. There may be something wrong with how we view the quest for happiness. Feeling fulfilled is the result of what we do for ourselves. It results from having a healthy amount of self-esteem and an awareness of what is personally satisfying and meaningful. Our mate can be a companion on that journey, but cannot be the ultimate source of gratification. To believe he or she can be is to indulge an expectation that is not only unrealistic but ultimately self-defeating.

Myth #12
Being a full-time wife and mother is a waste of potential.

Opting to stay at home and be a full-time wife and mother has, in recent years, been linked to a fear of independence. Full-time motherhood was not viewed as a free choice but rather one motivated by fear, by the anxiety associated with assertiveness and independence. The truth is that it is as easy to hide in the workplace as it is to hide at home, and a full-time wife and mother can indeed have chosen her role freely.

Too many women feel guilty because they prefer to remain at home and devote their time to raising a family. They have been made to feel that this role is somehow less meaningful and important than the role they could have chosen in the work world. The intrinsic value of the work experience has been greatly exaggerated.

"I bought the whole message, hook, line, and sinker," Penny explains. "I went to law school, passed the bar, and joined a large law firm. I entertained thoughts of marriage, but motherhood seemed absolutely remote. Then all of a sudden I found someone, fell in love, got married, and became pregnant. It all happened so fast. I'd always felt motherhood was something that happens to other people—something that women do when they don't have anything more important to accomplish. Lately, I've had to take a fresh look at issues that seemed so clear when I was single. My husband would love it if I would stay home and be a full-time mother— part of me wants that too in the worst way, and another part feels very guilty. I love my work, and I certainly don't want to waste the time and effort I've put into it."

Doubts about the timing and importance of motherhood plague not only career-directed women but also women who have chosen a more traditional homemaking role. Lois, the mother of two bright and active children, experiences a different kind of pressure surrounding motherhood. Shortly before her first child was born, Lois quit work after countless hours of discussion with her husband about income, life-style, and parenting. The decision to be a full-time mother was made long ago, but it hasn't been without recurrent nagging questions and doubts. Lois tells us, "Most of the time I really do know I made the right decision. There simply is no way I could have done the good job I've done with the kids if I'd also had to worry about working. But sometimes when people ask me what I do or when I see other women doing things that seem exciting, I wonder."

Being a full-time wife and mother and running a household well is an incredibly complicated and demanding job. Being able to be at home with one's children—seeing them off to school in the morning and being there when they come home from school in the afternoon—really allows a mother to have a more continuous experience with the child. The amount of attention to detail in parenting is tremendous—keeping track of what children eat, what they didn't eat, when they're due to go to the dentist, what time soccer practice is, who their friends are. These details combine to create the parent/child experience. Certainly the child who lives in a household where the mother has the opportunity to be at home has that experience in a more complete way.

The choices that women have to make today are probably more difficult than ever before. Many women who felt guilty about their wish to have children went to work and found their jobs to be not all that rewarding. Other women have pulled back from their commitment to work and have shifted from full-time to part-time employment or have arranged to do their work at home so they can spend more time with their children. But whatever the choices, it is significant that the importance of motherhood is being reevaluated today.

Myth #13
A good marriage should always be fair and equal.

As children we were all taught about fairness. Growing up, we believed that fairness existed in some real, tangible way even though we probably experienced many examples of unfair behavior. When we married, we expected our husband or wife, perhaps more than anyone else, to be fair to us. Kind and sensitive to us, too, but fair first of all, in the way that we had come to interpret fair. Unfortunately, this is more a hopeful wish than reality.

We are all disappointed, even hurt, when we first learn that fairness doesn't really exist in love and marriage. The truth is that relationships don't automatically find some natural equitable balance. Instead they tend to be out of balance. Typically one of the partners wants closeness and intimacy more than the other does. And typically one loves the other more than he or she is loved in return. Such imbalances can be seen as unfair, and certainly they are, but that doesn't change them.

"I'm always the one who's more physically

affectionate," says Arthur. "I usually make the first moves, take her hand, snuggle up to her in bed, rub her back, and initiate some kind of sexual contact. Sometimes that feels lousy because I'm left with a feeling that she doesn't care as much about me, that she's not as attracted to me as I am to her. It doesn't strike me as being fair that I am always the one expected to be the giver." Although Arthur is probably right—he does tend to be more generous than his mate—he does not understand the differences between himself and the woman he loves. He has a greater need for contact, a greater need for affection and tenderness, than his wife does. That doesn't make her wrong and him right; that doesn't make him the hero and her the villain. It simply means that the two of them are different. He is not aware that there may be some normal differences between the two of them that have nothing to do with the depth of their love or even the quality of their relationship.

How many times have you thought, "I wouldn't do that to my spouse"? Most of us are highly sensitized to the inequities we see in our relationships, but we have a blind spot when it comes to seeing ourselves engaging in behavior that is unfair.

"He's a lot more critical than I am," says Harriet. "If I'm really honest with myself I don't think that he reacts more negatively to what I do than I react to what he does. But it does strike me as unfair that he has to put everything into words while I keep my petty little annoyances to myself." Obviously Harriet feels that she's being "fairer" than her husband because she edits her critical remarks and he doesn't. The difficulty is that there is really nothing wrong with either one of these positions. Some individuals tend to be more openly critical and some tend to keep many dissatisfactions to themselves. Basically what's involved in any marriage is an adjustment to tremendous individual differences in styles of relating. We have a tendency in marriage to want to reduce differences by making our mate respond, feel, and react just as we do. Often what we were most attracted to in a mate was what was different, and yet when we get married that is frequently the first thing we systematically try to stamp out.

We need to put our notions of fairness on the shelf and realize that we can actually expect to find fairness in our day-to-day existence with our mate. What we need to develop is not a scorecard for "who did what to whom" but some sense of acceptance.

Dwelling on inequities does nothing but foster cold, angry, and resentful self-righteousness in ourselves and guilt and a sad sense of inadequacy in our mate. None of these feelings, ours or our mate's, is constructive or has any chance of leading to a positive result.

Usually what we consider to be fair and equitable is something that we can provide and bring to the relationship with relative comfort and ease. The truth is that what we may be asking may be easy for us but very difficult for our mate. For example, you may think, "It's not fair for me to be open and vulnerable and expressive and for you to be more closed and unwilling to express your feelings." Being open and expressive is extremely easy for some people and obviously very difficult for others.

Fairness has nothing to do with a good relationship. Most of us simply are being who we are, and if we love each other and can accept each other that should be sufficient.

Myth #14
A woman or man can be devoted fully to work, family, and marriage.

The traditional family has always involved a division of labor. In ancient times the man was the hunter and the woman was the keeper of the hearth. They complemented each other. The family really functioned as a miniature economy with each person incredibly dependent on the other for survival itself. During those times no one dared to try to "do it all," for everyone had plenty to do with his or her separate job.

How times have changed. Now we try to do it all, and do it all well—committing ourselves fully to work, being a good mate, being an excellent parent. This notion of doing it all didn't develop out of nowhere. It evolved out of the social upheavals of the last twenty years. Women saw men as being able to devote themselves fully to education and career development and yet they were still husbands and fathers. So women adopted men as a kind of model and moved into the workplace to demonstrate their ability to achieve and compete on an equal basis.

The truth is that men were able to "do it all" for one simple reason—they had wives. Women forgot that critical element and found out, much to their chagrin, that it really is impossible to do everything well. Certainly men don't do everything well either. A man who devotes himself fully to work does so only at the expense of taking away time, energy, and attention from his family; the man who tries to have some kind of balance in his life and be an attentive husband and devoted father tends not to be a high achiever in his career. People who attempt to master the three areas of work, marriage, and family end up exhausted and frustrated. Something has to give.

Most recently, women are experimenting with doing it all not simultaneously but sequentially. While this may seem like a serious compromise, it does allow a woman to do something well without feeling guilty. Men typically don't feel the same strain and pressure to do all three things well. The mandate that men have been given historically is to achieve in the workplace. If a man feels he is doing that well, he is likely to feel little guilt if the price tag includes evening meetings, business trips, and missed activities with his children. Women, on the other hand, tend to get caught up in the bind of working, coming home, and shouldering the responsibility of more than their share of household tasks in addition to maintaining some kind of career. Women can't juggle all these well because the responsibilities are physically impossible to juggle, and so they tend to feel guilty, unlike their male counterparts.

It would seem that "doing it all" is a myth in marriage that we could very well do without. We have only so much time and energy, and it's important to set priorities. There is no way that men or women can spread themselves so thin without potential problems. All of us need to assess our values and priorities.

Myth #15
If you have to "work" on a marriage, something is wrong.

When we fall in love and decide to get married we tend to think it is going to be easier than it turns out to be. In actuality, no matter how much we love each other, marriage is not only wonderful, but also predictably very difficult. We may have learned geometry in school, but we weren't taught how to love. We may have learned how to be successful in our jobs, but most of us have had less success in our relationships. There is probably no more complicated and challenging a task than taking on a long-term relationship.

Good relationships don't simply happen; they are a direct product of the energy, time, and work that we put into them. The only kind of relationship that doesn't require work is one that's not worth having. In the context of marriage, "work" has gotten kind of a black eye. The mythology is that if you have to work at a marriage, it wasn't good enough to begin with. The truth is that all marriages, at times, require special efforts and heightened sensitivities. Working on a relationship allows it to develop a direction that suits the needs of both partners. In the absence of work, husbands and wives passively watch fate and conflicting expectations take their toll.

So what is work? Work is not talking a relationship to death, it is treating one's mate differently. Working on a relationship really involves personal change. We need to be willing to be more responsive to what our mate needs from us, and we need to be able to change ourselves as well.

Many people feel that they are working on a relationship when in reality they are simply sitting around and blaming their mates for their personal dissatisfaction. Blaming and complaining do not constitute work and rarely have anything to do with providing a partner with new information. More often they are used as weapons to punish a mate.

Working on a marriage is an integral part of any sound bond between a husband and wife, and the idea that it is unnecessary is one of the most deadly marital myths. Couples should understand and accept that there will be rough times in their relationship, but these rough times do not mean the marriage is a failure.

LETTING GO OF SELF-DEFEATING BELIEFS

All of the myths we have explored are in some degree part of the belief system of most married couples. Whether we are conscious of them or not, they function as implicit expectations for us in our relationships. What they all have in common is that they are unrealistic, based more on wish than reality, and, most important, that they are self-defeating.

Even those husbands and wives who know better rarely question the underlying beliefs that govern what they want and hope to get out of their marriage. Rarer still are those who grapple with the real truth of relationships and what is realistic. This failure to revise our thinking comes not from laziness but rather from a false kind of security. None of us is really that open to change unless we are convinced we must be. And, unfortunately, our society continues to tell us that the ideal is possible, that having it all is a noble goal instead of what it really is, a trap that fixates our minds on fantasy rather than realities which ultimately can offer more.

It is always difficult to let go of idealistic notions that promise easy gratification. Initially, couples who come to grips with their unrealistic expectations feel a sense of loss. It is almost akin to a loss of innocence. The anticipation of this loss is what keeps husbands and wives from letting go of myths. They don't realize that the rewards of letting go are far greater than those of hanging on.

In thinking about each of these myths, ask yourself what might happen if you began thinking differently. Don't let yourself be disheartened at first, for that is a normal and understandable response. Ask yourself: What am I really letting go of? Aren't these myths the very beliefs that have really led me down a path of increasing disillusionment?

The next set of awarenesses that will come to you will undoubtedly be feelings of independence and Self-Directedness that will actually make you feel stronger, more in control of your own destiny.

Those who cling tenaciously to these myths fail to understand a fundamental truth about change in marriage: there must be a void created for any new patterns to be established. And releasing one's mate from the burden of having to meet unrealistic expectations allows him or her to perceive you in a new way and to think about being different on his or her own terms.

In working with couples, we have found that coming to grips with mythical beliefs about marriage, while initially sobering, actually provides a framework in which they discover more acceptance and greater intimacy. Recognizing the presence of these beliefs is a prerequisite to changing the marriage system. Most couples find it a relief to unburden themselves of expectations that have only led to disappointment and disenchantment. Taking a fresh look at the promise of marriage is the only antidote to the feelings of disappointment pervading so many marriages today.

CHAPTER THREE

Change: Having an Impact

Over the past twenty years we have systematically been encouraged by the culture to look outside of ourselves for solutions to a wide range of problems. When attitudes, prejudices, and fears proved to be resistant to change, we looked to Congress, the courts, even civil disobedience as instruments of change. This is obviously appropriate if the problem to be addressed is an external one. The difficulty is that we have over-generalized the problem-solving process, tending to see all dilemmas and their solutions as essentially external to us as individuals. We have even made the mistake of applying this solution to problems in marriage—"It's their fault!" is the most common conclusion. When it comes to relationships we all tend to shirk personal responsibility.

The fact is that many of us are Other-Directed

in our marriages. There are, however, concrete steps we can take to understand our Other-Directedness and become more Self-Directed.

One of the myths we've discussed is that our mates would lovingly correct their faults if only they had more information about how we felt and the effect their faults had upon us. The process of supplying this information we called *communication*, and we deified it. But communication isn't simply information. Over a period of time it's much more likely to become information glut. As most of us use it, communication has degenerated into a sanctioned form of nagging, complaining, and manipulation—which doesn't work and doesn't solve the problem.

The only effective method of changing the marriage system is an internal and personal one which is quite unrelated to demanding change in our partner's conduct. Most people can't bear the thought of having to give up pushing their mate to be different even though in their hearts they know their pushing has consistently met with failure. We're afraid that if we don't keep pushing, nothing will happen and we will be forever trapped in a static and hopeless state of vague disenchantment. But to the contrary, when we abandon useless attempts to change our mate and instead focus on ourselves, changes surprisingly and automatically begin to occur in the marriage system!

Change in a marriage is possible, but it will never happen so long as you make it something your mate should be doing. The Other-Directed approach, employing communication and negotiations based on blame and the shifting of responsibility to one's partner, invariably creates even more conflict rather than resolving it. Most marriage counselors employ this same Other-Directed, interactive model while working with couples. And it is for this reason that marriage counseling so often fails, leaving people even more pessimistic than they were before they sought professional help. After all, if the frank expression of feelings, the bargaining back and forth, and the attempts at compromise didn't offer any change or relief, what would? We are all too familiar with endless talks that ultimately lead to frustration, disappointment, even ultimatums and threats of divorce. It is never too late for change to occur, but it will occur only when we examine marital problems from an entirely different perspective.

REMEMBERING THE GOOD TIMES

Anyone who stays married wants the experience to be as happy as possible. But motivation is not enough. None of us has the energy to initiate a process of change unless we have hope that it will lead to greater fulfillment. With respect to marriage, we must believe things can be richer, better. They can! As evidence of this potential, we need only examine the beginnings of our relationship. Unfortunately, most of us fall prey to the mistaken belief that what is happening now in the marriage is all that is real and what happened in the past is just a wistful and pleasant memory. In our most cynical moments we even think those earlier times must only have been fantasies. But the truth is that the way we were with each other in the beginning of our marriage was very real and represented a time when our love was both genuine and generous. It was a time of fewer expectations, a time when we gave freely and cherished our mate and, in turn, felt accepted and valued. The past was a time when there was more listening and less complaining, greater forgiveness and less self-involvement, more love and less hurt.

Most couples had good reasons for getting married in the first place. Each thought the other person was wonderful and hoped he or she would think that forever. Whatever our level of maturity when we married, and irrespective of how well we really knew the other person, most of us married because we found someone so important and valuable to us that we wanted to intertwine our lives.

Try to remember that you are still those same two people who once stood together and spoke vows of love and commitment. Whatever changes you have gone through and however you may have caused each other pain, take a moment and look back, recalling the love you both enjoyed.

Being willing to remember and to reconnect with those feelings is absolutely critical, for it is those very experiences that provide a measure of the potential you share. Even if those feelings have long been overlaid, remembering why you married and how you felt provides a beacon for the path back—not back to the past, for that is gone forever, but back to the aliveness and hope you once felt and can feel in the future.

You may be thinking, "But we're both so different now—there's no way we could ever feel the way we used to about each other." The truth is that you are probably a lot less different than you may believe and a whole lot closer to feelings of warmth, trust, and caring. But what we are asking requires an act of faith in the beginning—a willingness to trust that the possibility of reestablishing clear and positive feelings of love exists.

"It's been so long since either one of us has felt anything like what you're talking about," a woman said skeptically when asked to recall some of her earlier feelings about her marriage. But when encouraged to try, she began recounting stories from their courtship, and before long she was smiling and speaking with warm animation about how, against both parents' wishes, they eloped. Reconnecting with the importance and meaning of a mate doesn't automatically wipe away hurt and disappointment, but it does provide a starting point.

ARE YOU OTHER-DIRECTED IN YOUR MARRIAGE?

Most of us are not good observers of ourselves or our marriages. It's easier to imagine how we would like to be than to see clearly how we really are. We can objectively analyze our friends' marriages, and we can accurately pinpoint our mate's every weakness and imperfection, but when it comes to ourselves we seem to have a blind spot. This blindness is natural and it protects us from excessive self-criticism, but it can also lead to conflict and tension in a relationship.

"She takes everything I do for granted," laments a man about his marriage. "I feel important only insofar as I make her happy. I keep thinking that she will recognize how I try to show my love, but the more I do, the more she expects and the less she gives back." He obviously thinks that the problem is all hers, but he couldn't be more wrong. He feels most comfortable when he is needed. He hides his disappointment behind a mask of slightly martyred silence when he is perceived as the "good guy." He is in pain, but it is easier for him to tolerate that than to move toward Self-Directedness—to take the risk of making appropriate demands, being a bit tougher, and showing some of the feelings he secretly holds inside. He would rather complain indirectly and feel self-righteous than ever say no. Recognizing what we do that leads to conflict and tension requires our taking personal responsibility for it—something most of us are loath to do.

Many of us don't see very clearly how Other-Directed we are in the conduct of our marriages. The following are seven critical signs that reflect Other-Directedness:

1. *SECRET BLAME.* This involves a belief, whether expressed or not, that your major marital conflicts are related specifically to your mate's behavior. The emphasis here is upon how *your mate* acts rather than how *you* act. You hold your mate responsible for the problems in your marriage and feel victimized by him or her.

2. *OVERT COMPLAINTS.* Being Other-Directed always means making complaints. Sometimes we may think we are simply making observations when, in fact, we are really subtly expressing disappointment and dissatisfaction. Even though you may not see yourself as complaining, does your mate see you as such? "You always," "You never," and "You don't care about how I feel" are the obvious telltale words. Less obvious but equally telling is how you talk about your mate to your friends. The Other-Directed person often burdens friends with complaints about the mate's shortcomings.

3. *ANALYZING ONE'S PARTNER.* We all are interested in why other people act and feel the way they do, but Other-Directed people are truly fascinated. They spend a lot of energy endlessly analyzing their mate's behavior rather than coming to grips with their own.

4. *FEELINGS OF ANGER AND VICTIMIZATION.* Other-Directed individuals hang on to accumulated anger and resentment. They say they feel the way they do because of their mate's treatment of them, and often they feel subtly victimized by their circumstances. Such people, for instance, may lament waking up yet one more dreary morning with an out-of-control alcoholic, wondering what they did to deserve such a rotten situation and hating their mate for making their life so miserable. But at the same time they are blind to what is making them stay in such a destructive relationship.

5. *FANTASIZING A BETTER PARTNER.* Since Other-Directed individuals believe their mate is the culprit in any marital disharmony, it is easy for them to believe that a new partner is the logical solution. They can rationalize affairs, whether real or only wishful thinking, because the problem with their marriage is "out there."

6. *SELF-RIGHTEOUSNESS.* A sure sign of Other-Directedness is a conviction that your feelings are "right" and your reactions justified. Being right is an empty victory, for even if you are right, your rightness is irrelevant to any positive change in the marriage. Your being right isn't going to change your mate for the better—it will simply make him or her feel deficient.

7. *FEELINGS OF HOPELESSNESS.* When we allow our sense of ease and well-being to be determined primarily by our mate's feelings and reactions, the single most predictable outcome is a terrible sense of powerlessness. When we repeatedly try to get our mate to change and he or she consistently thwarts our efforts and disappoints us, we gradually begin to feel hopeless.

Consider these signs of Other-Directedness and see if they occur in your own conduct with your mate. Focus attention only on your own feelings and reactions and not on those of your mate. The first step in regaining power over your marriage experience is to realize how much control over your happiness you have unwittingly placed in the hands of your partner.

WHY YOUR MATE
RESISTS CHANGE

When accusations are hurled at you, it's likely that you feel inadequate, guilty, and resentful—and also, of course, somewhat stubborn. The same goes for your mate.

We assume that our partner's refusal to change is a reflection of his or her lack of concern, but much of the time that is just not true. Most married people don't set out to make their mates unhappy, and they certainly don't derive some perverse pleasure from continually thwarting them.

It isn't lack of love for the other person that makes it difficult to change. Often it's lack of self-confidence. For example, the man who is unimaginative and constricted sexually may not be uncaring at all; he may just be too shy to act any other way. The woman who retreats from intimate communications with her husband may do so not because she doesn't feel love for him but rather because closeness and intimacy make her anxious and uneasy.

Though psychologically understandable, a mate's lack of self-confidence and consequent self-protective behavior can still be quite disruptive to the marriage. Many of the things we react to negatively in a mate may be painful and difficult for him or her to change because they are basic and often unconscious self-protective strategies, but we don't see them that way; we take them personally.

Verbal attacks only push people into a rigid and defensive stance. When we are under attack, we are certainly not open to change. Blame does nothing but underscore growing feelings of displeasure, and perhaps even more important, it effectively blocks any real possibility for enriching one's marriage. Conversely, when we feel loved and accepted, we are more receptive to the notion of modifying our behavior. We can then start to think in terms of self-directedness.

BECOMING SELF-DIRECTED

Becoming Self-Directed in marriage requires realizing that we, each in our own way, are responsible for the soundness and vitality of our relationship. This realization is a process that takes time. It will feel unfamiliar and lonely, requiring no small measure of faith on your part. But if you have the courage to take the following steps, it will work.

1. *MAKING A COMMITMENT.* Understanding what is going on in your marriage doesn't come out of dialogues with your mate; it is something you discover within yourself. And in the course of that inner search you must face difficult questions. How willing are you to take the responsibility for feeling whole and worth-

while independent of your marriage? How willing are you to stop complaining and start doing something different? How much work and energy and commitment are you willing to put into the marriage? Most of us try to avoid these questions and the dangerous ground they explore. They make us feel alone.

Liz and Reggie have been married for twelve years. Both consider the marriage to be basically strong and satisfying, although both have complaints focusing on issues of closeness and intimacy. "I wish he were more open with me," Liz says. "It's like prying the lid off a can to get him to talk about us and how he feels about me. I know he cares, but I sure wouldn't mind hearing about it a little more often." Reggie sees things a bit differently. "She's always telling me she'd like me to talk more and be more expressive. The truth is, she doesn't really want me to be more open about everything, just about how I feel about her. It's all right for her to have insecurities, but she doesn't want to hear about mine."

The truth is that Liz does give off mixed signals about her wish for openness on Reggie's part. Does she really want him to be more revealing? Why? Is it to understand him better and feel closer to him through that understanding? Or is it to reassure herself of her value to him? Does she want exposure on his part or simply expressions of his love? Does her view of him as tight-lipped actually compel him to be tight-lipped? Does she tell Reggie she wants complete openness while at the same time communicating to him that she can't handle any sign of uncertainty or wavering confidence on his part? These are some of the questions Liz needs to ask herself. It's so much easier to point the finger at our partner and tell him or her to change than it is to understand ourselves well enough to know why we want him or her to change. Being responsible always involves the willingness—and the courage—to take a good hard look at ourselves.

We don't like to feel alone with our problems. So many of us avoid that feeling by seeing the problems not in ourselves but in our mate. But standing alone can make us stronger, not weaker. When we overcome our fear of standing alone we create an opportunity for change to occur—we don't feel victimized or helpless, we are ready to do and be something different.

2. *CONTAINING AND DISENGAGING.* The next step in moving toward Self-Directedness requires you to stop blaming and complaining, give up feeling

victimized and hopeless, put any residual anger or resentment on hold, and stop indulging in the thought that there is someone better out there. These are powerful thoughts and feelings that need to be set aside. They can be contained when you deliberately choose not to express them and prepare to disengage. It's really not quite as difficult as you might think, and right away you will begin to feel more powerful, for you will be exercising choice and sparing yourself disappointment.

The process of disengaging involves temporarily not holding your mate responsible for your feelings or for whatever tension or conflict exists in the marriage. To do this requires a kind of emotional separation that should not be made in anger and should not even be discussed with your mate. You simply stand back and detach yourself from seeing your mate as either providing or withholding whatever contributes to your sense of well-being. By suspending your dependency upon your mate you will find a new reliance upon yourself as the chief source of personal fulfillment.

3. *TAKING THE INITIATIVE.* Once you have stood back a bit from the relationship, you will notice that the resentments

you may have been accumulating over the years slowly melt away. Holding your mate responsible for your feelings is the core cause of resentment, and freeing your mate from that responsibility has the effect of freeing you from pent-up anger and disappointment. A wonderful by-product of this release is a greatly heightened sense of acceptance of your mate. Now that you are acting more as an initiator in the marriage and less as a reactor, try experimenting with taking on more personal responsibility. For example, try behaving as if you were responsible for creating friendship, passion, and family harmony. Then assume the responsibility for how conflicts and fights are handled. Try giving unselfishly. This means giving up scorekeeping and becoming generous and loving without calling a whole lot of attention to your actions. Above all, focus upon actions rather than words and relate to your mate from the perspective of care, generosity, acceptance, and personal security. Do these things with patience and consistency and your marriage cannot help but be transformed.

ACTIONS RATHER THAN WORDS

We can have impact, but with deeds rather than words. It is our actions that have effect, not our stated wishes. The marriage system is as highly choreographed as an intricate dance step. Our partners can do what they do only because we are doing what we do. If we change the step, so must they—if we dare to be different, then they must be different too. We are only helpless as long as we insist upon behaving in the same old and familiar ways. Power comes not from trying to make our mate different but from developing the courage and responsibility to be different ourselves.

"I never thought about the passage of time, because I felt good about myself. But all of a sudden, I've become aware of my age, and I feel totally at loose ends." Brook, at 43, has been married for most of her adult life. She married Glen, an airline pilot, shortly after he came back from Vietnam, when she was 24. His work schedule over the years made it necessary for him to be out of town much of the time, which was all right with her, since she focused her attention and energy on her children. The trouble began when the last child went off to college a year ago. "I was forced to look at our marriage, and I was appalled at what I saw," Brook continued. "I realized I had gradually pulled away from Glen because it was easier to feel needed by the kids. When I tried to redirect all that intensity back toward Glen, everything went downhill. I wanted him to make up for the loss I felt. After all, he was the one who was gone all the time, and I expected him to help me feel wanted. I mean, isn't that what a husband is for? All I wanted was a little more time and attention.''

The truth is that Brook wanted a whole lot more than just a little time and attention, for her husband willingly gave her that. What she really needed was a new source of validation and meaning, and she began relentlessly searching for it in the marriage. She didn't realize that she was much more resentful of Glen's absence than she ever admitted to herself and had angrily withdrawn from him and given herself to the children. Her behavior over the years had inadvertently blocked any real closeness between the two of them. Then when she turned toward Glen and wanted him to meet her needs for more intensity in their relationship, Brook fell into a pattern of angry complaints. Although Glen tried to make an effort to spend more time together, she continued to feel frustrated and unfulfilled.

She sought counseling, and it was suggested to her that she examine some of the basic and largely unconscious beliefs which shaped her expectations about Glen. She soon understood that she looked to him to solve personal concerns that were essentially hers alone. Reluctantly at first, she began doing things alone, reading more, exploring classes and other involvements, and—most important—doing these things without resentment. Feeling less criticized and pressured, Glen slowly began to move closer to her and enjoy the contact. It wasn't until Brook realized she, and she alone, was responsible for the meaning and importance in her life that her marriage began to change.

Individuals such as Brook fail to realize that blaming depletes their energy and makes them feel powerless. When we believe it's our mate's fault, our mate then has all the power and we have none. Our fate, our self-esteem, and our happiness reside in our mate's hands. We are helpless to alter even the smallest and most inconsequential aspects of our situation if we insist upon holding our mate responsible.

Why would we willingly put ourselves in such a powerless position? Because we do not want the burden of responsibility. During times of upset and distress, most of us have been taught to look anywhere but within for the answers. Even as children nagged by our parents to do our homework, how many of us looked to ourselves and our procrastination as the cause of that nagging?

To change our marriage we must abandon our attempts to alter our partner's conduct and instead take the responsibility for altering our own. This single shift in orientation can produce dramatic changes within the marriage, because blame and accusation fall away. When we are not in the uncomfortable position of having to defend ourselves against accusations, we feel more accepted, relaxed, and receptive. Many husbands and wives find they can give only when it is not being demanded.

Some of you might be thinking, "But what about something as blatant as a mate who is having an affair? Isn't that the mate's fault and doesn't he or she have to change if the marriage is to survive?" The answer is yes and no. Yes, ultimately the affair must stop if the marriage is to continue in any meaningful way, but the real question is what will stop the affair. Telling your partner how awful the situation makes you feel won't do it, for that may very well be part of the game plan. Becoming anguished and enraged and begging your mate not to do it again won't work either unless guilt and pity are the primary goals. What does work is understanding the part you played in the creation of the situation, taking responsibility for it, and setting some firm limits. People stop having affairs when they are faced with potential loss, not simply of comfort but of love and the marriage itself. In such a situation, the answer may very well be finding the courage to say, "I won't put up with this affair, and I will survive with or without you." Personal responsibility, personal risk, and personal action form the foundation for any change and are the only choices that leave us feeling empowered rather than helpless and victimized.

THE COURAGE TO CHANGE

Change is scary. The truth is that change has as much to do with endings as new beginnings. Any important change demands that we leave behind a relatively comfortable and predictable way of being. There is a feeling of loss, which may be painful, but we cannot begin some new way of being without first closing off old attitudes or behaviors. At the very least these old ways of acting were familiar, which provided a modicum of comfort and safety.

The discomfort of change, however, is more than simply facing loss. If we really believed we could begin making changes successfully, the process would be relatively simple. What stands in the way of change is a list of imagined negative outcomes. For example, if we secretly know we are too dependent upon our mate, the antidote is to face our fears and explore ways of being more independent. But to do that requires letting go, even though we may be afraid that moving in that direction, rather than allowing us to feel better, will lead instead to a loss of intimacy and closeness.

To change we must take a leap of faith, believing in the possibility of change. We must behave differently and create new experiences not simply in our imaginations but in our real day-to-day existence with our mate. To do this, we must risk discomfort now for a payoff later.

For most of us, that feels something like stepping off a cliff into a void and not knowing what the outcome will be.

We need courage. Most of us wait for it to magically appear before we are willing to assume the risk. This is a mistake. Courage is a by-product of risk-taking—it comes after we've taken the chance to be different, never before. If we wait to feel courageous, we will never take risks, and never change. Our willingness to experiment with different ways of responding to our spouse is what produces the possibility of change.

Clark was 36 and had been married for eight years to an exceptionally strong and emotionally expressive woman. Her goal during any of their conflicts was to win her point, while Clark's was to keep the peace. It's not that he wouldn't have dearly loved to come out on top once in a while, for he would have, with a driving passion. It's just that his wish to win wasn't as strong as his fear of intense emotional conflict. In his public life as an attorney in the district attorney's office of a large city, he was aggressive and direct and won the respect of opposing counsel and judges alike for his competence. But in his personal life he was halting and inarticulate and was likely to say, "Yes, dear," whenever there was any potential conflict with his wife.

Not only did Clark hate to lose every disagreement, but his wife, Linda, hated to win every one. Secretly, she would have respected him more if he had stood up for himself and fought back. Clark tried to negotiate differences in a gentlemanly way, and Linda had all the finesse of a charging rhino. He was rational; she was tough as nails and capable of tossing below-the-belt epithets that dared him to assert his manhood. None of her rough behavior, however, was an indication that she did not love Clark; she was fiercely loyal to and supportive of him in all areas except those in which she was determined to get her way.

Clark had tried everything, or so he thought. He had carefully explained to her that her need for control was excessive, that her temper was hurtful, and that if she could only see what it felt like to be on the receiving end of her outbursts, she would surely change. All his talking had no effect other than to make her feel a bit guilty.

Nothing changed until Clark gave up seeing Linda as the problem and addressed the real culprit—himself. Clark was terrified of anger, having grown up with an out-of-control and occasionally violent alcoholic father. He was afraid that if he expressed angry feelings, he would create the same frightening scenes he had witnessed as a child at home. He had thought many times to himself, "I've held so much in—if I ever let it out I don't know what would happen."

Essentially, the danger for Clark wasn't in

expressing his anger but in continuing to hide it. He backed away from confronting Linda to avoid dealing with his own feelings of growing anger. And Linda knew it. His timidity with her was like a red flag she constantly charged, trying to get some sort of reaction from him she could trust.

Clark came to understand that if he wanted Linda to be different he had to change. She couldn't behave in the way she typically did unless he cooperated and played out his timid role. The realization that he wasn't simply tolerating her bombastic style but actively encouraging it came to him as a shock.

What Clark realized was that his problem was not really his wife's style of dealing with conflict but rather his own. That realization created the first opportunity for meaningful change. That is the first step for all of us—coming to the awareness that if anything is going to happen it is up to us.

Having assumed that personal responsibility, we automatically feel less helpless, more powerful, but also a bit more anxious. Our wish to stay in our emotional "comfort zone"—however natural—is the single most critical impediment to change. But if we do stay there, we merely buy a little time and pay the price of even greater discomfort down the road. If we avoid the challenges and difficulties of coming to grips with those aspects of our personality that are self-defeating, we eventually sabotage our own marriage.

Understanding that we must be the one to change leads us to decide what exactly it is that we need to change. Clark needed to find a more constructive way to handle and express feelings of anger. It meant that he had to stop trying to avoid them and begin dealing with them in a more effective way.

CONSTRUCTIVE ATTEMPTS AT CHANGE

You may be thinking that the positions we've taken on communication, negotiation, and change are extreme. In a way they are. But they are also the only effective way we've found to consistently keep a marriage on track.

But aren't there some communications that are fruitful and constructive? Certainly. While we've described some of the common pitfalls of communication, we don't want to leave you with the impression that all attempts at changing one's mate are bad, for they are not. We are not advocating quiet marriages. Our attempt is not to silence you but to alert you to certain self-defeating patterns into which marriage easily falls.

What then are the guidelines for how we talk to each other and explain our feelings, needs, and reactions? Let's take a look at the following chart:

COMMUNICATION

CONSTRUCTIVE	DESTRUCTIVE
Informative	Accusatory
Elaborative	Repetitive
Vulnerable/revealing	Defensive/withholding
Observation-driven	Security-driven

Communication is the single most important tool we use to create and sustain intimacy. It is by no means dominated by words and includes the whole range of our nonverbal behavior and actions toward one another. The "message" is the basic unit of communication. And people are pretty smart—the real message gets through regardless of how we may wish at times to disguise it. We may use words to indicate one thing while a sigh or tone of voice betrays us, allowing the true message to be sent. Whatever we intend to communicate—perhaps a promise, perhaps an apology—the ultimate meaning of the message is embedded in our actions.

Constructive communication is informative, not condemning, demanding, belittling, or accusatory. Informative statements are personal declarations. Personal declarations typically begin with the word *I*, while judgmental statements typically begin with the word *you*.

Healthy marital communication is elaborative. As we speak to each other, our next sentence is usually designed to elaborate—to fill in the gaps or reduce the ambiguity of what we've just said. In a way, communication is one long string of "in other words . . ." But there is a great difference between elaboration and repetition. Most of us fall into the deadly trap of repetition. Much of what passes as marital communication is simply chewing endlessly on something old and essentially critical. How much of what we say to our mate is new and how much just rephrasing various old themes of disappointment?

The trick is to catch our repetitions and do something different. Sure, a certain amount of redundancy is necessary, but we all know when what we say isn't being heard or is being disregarded. It is human nature to think that perhaps the problem is that we haven't stated our point clearly enough or underscored just how important it is to us. Wrong on both counts—we've been heard, but disregarded. Plaintive complaints about a husband's excessive drinking, however legitimate they may be, typically go disregarded. What will be regarded is something like "The next time you stay out drinking all night, I won't be here when you come home."

We repeat complaints when we feel victimized and make our mate solely responsible for the solution to our discomfort. We communicate constructively when we directly assume the responsibility for coming up with a solution that involves something we will do, not something our mate must do.

Constructive marital exchanges are revealing.

They expose us, make us vulnerable. We can't be or feel close unless we can find the courage to expose those aspects of ourselves we typically don't show the rest of the world. Destructive communication is withholding and defensive. One of the most common marital communications involves batting accusations and criticism back and forth, being defensive and withholding. Listen to the following dialogue:

SHE: How dare you say my mother isn't welcome in my own house?

HE: I didn't say she wasn't welcome, and it's *our* house.

SHE: So what? Are you calling me a liar? That's exactly what you said.

HE: I did not. What I said was that with everything that's going on now, I didn't think the timing was all that good.

SHE: Well, that's what you meant. I know you don't like her. You don't even have to like her, she's my mother.

HE: I never said I didn't like her. I just don't feel all that comfortable with her. Besides, you're not so terrific when my parents come to visit either.

SHE: I can't believe it—this is so typical. Now we're talking about you and your feelings. At least when my mother comes she's helpful and

doesn't sit around expecting to be
waited on.

HE: No, she comes in and takes over.
Where do you think you learned
your 'everything has to be my way'
routine?

This is not communication but just an opportunity to air a lot of old gripes. How different
might it have been if it had begun more like:

HE: I know how important it is for you
to have your mom come this weekend, but I'm under a lot of pressure and I've got a deadline on that
project. How about if you invite
her next weekend?

Or:

SHE: I know it's not easy for you having my mother around the house,
but I really want to see her. Think
about it and give me a time in the
next couple of weeks when it would
be easiest for you.

To do this obviously takes caring and a willingness to prevent anger from building. It is
only when we feel good about each other that
we can communicate with any kind of clarity
and sensitivity. In the first dialogue example,
the issue wasn't the wife's mother coming to

visit; it was hurt, misunderstanding, and resentment. That was what the couple should have been talking about, for until those issues are resolved, all their communication will be tinged by those feelings. Constructive communication reassures and promotes acceptance, while destructive marital talking demands change.

What if we give up trying to tell our mate to change? What if instead we try actively to want our mate to do and be what he or she wants? But, you might point out, my mate is wrong. My mate should not do what he or she does. My mate is unfair. And you might very well be right, but you are the one who is unhappy, who feels so frustrated by your mate's unwillingness to change, who feels so victimized. Acceptance is an active process, something we learn to do. It is wanting our mate to be essentially the way he or she is.

WHEN IT SEEMS INTOLERABLE

But what about change when it is really necessary? Aren't there things people do that are clearly wrong? Certainly this is true. There is an old Zen saying: "Reality is only unacceptable when it's unacceptable." This pretty much holds true for problems or flaws we see in our mates.

Problems fall into two broad groups: acceptable and unacceptable. Unfortunately, no one can tell us into which category problems should be assigned, for that is highly subjective.

Let's first take a look at "acceptable" problems— those petty annoyances that plague every marriage and are largely due to our differing personalities. Typically, these difficulties are resolved by negotiating and compromise. But, as we've mentioned, certain things are not really negotiable, and continued efforts at change lead to frustration on the part of the "changer" and irritation and feelings of deficiency on the part of the "changee." A good way to determine whether an issue is negotiable is to count the number of negotiations that have taken place. Five seems to be a pretty good cut-off number. With less than five you may not have made your point emphatically enough or allowed for natural resistance to change. More than five and you can assume you are being unheard or ignored even though your partner may acknowledge with words the correctness of your position and his or her willingness to be different. More than five negotiations simply wastes time and energy and will only lead to resentment— yours and your mate's.

So what do you do when you have one of these "acceptable" problems and your mate won't change? There are only two choices. Either accept the flaw and let it gradually melt into the background, or go on badgering and harassing your partner. There is absolutely no payoff with the latter.

Accepting flaws means not taking them personally. It means putting them in a larger perspective, taking your mate "for better or worse." An inability to tolerate flaws that are merely annoying—that are really "acceptable"—inevitably makes a marriage frustrating and disappointing. If you look at your mate and focus constantly on the negative, you will never see the whole person.

What about unacceptable problems—those situations that are clearly impossible in any marriage? First of all, compromise and negotiation don't work with such problems and are not appropriate. The woman whose husband is physically or verbally abusive to her doesn't alter those patterns through any process of negotiation. The man who discovers that his wife is abusing drugs or is an alcoholic doesn't change that behavior through compromise.

The only communication that has even the slightest chance of changing unacceptable problems is an ultimatum. An ultimatum need not be delivered in anger. Rather, it can be made with great concern and caring. But an ultimatum can never be an empty threat; you must mean it and be willing to follow through. If you deliver an ultimatum you must be willing to face being alone.

Let's take a clear-cut example of an ultimatum delivered by someone who has reached a breaking point with an alcoholic mate: "I love you, but I'm not willing to live with you anymore as long as you continue drinking. If you will get professional help and join AA, I will stay and give you whatever support you need. If you choose not to, I am going to leave you." This is clearly an ultimatum, but one that carries with it compassion and concern.

Obviously one ultimatum we advise is insisting on marital counseling. While there is no magic cure for what ails a marriage, most problems that are viewed as unacceptable are rarely resolved except in the presence of a third party who can function as a mediator, a clarifier, and a facilitator. If your mate will not go with you, you can start by yourself and then later, with your counselor's guidance, suggest just one visit together. We advise one visit because most people will never see a psychotherapist or counselor if they believe they have to continue going. After that one visit, more will typically follow.

TAKING YOUR MATE OFF THE HOOK

Sometimes in marriage, positive feelings seem so much a part of the past that we question the very existence of love in the present relationship. Rather than ease, affection, and positive regard, we may feel only anger and frustration toward our mate, or from our mate. Either way, such feelings are painful and profoundly disappointing. We tend to see negative feelings as the antithesis of love, but in actuality they are often a mask we hide behind. Even so cold and seemingly barren a response as emotional indifference may be a defense against the risk of active caring. We hide away our feelings and put on our angry or impassive faces not to express a lack of caring, but frequently to protect ourselves from caring too much, from expecting too much and being disappointed.

Stepping into the breech and assuming the responsibility for being the agent of change also means accepting the consequences, the good and the bad, of who your mate is. This is the person you chose, and that choice was made for positive reasons that are inextricably tangled up with some negative traits. When we begin to let each other be the people we are, we begin to feel the sense of acceptance we so enjoyed early in the relationship. The more accepted we feel, the more likely we are to give, not out of duty or guilt but out of a wish to return the gift of acceptance and renewed friendship.

When we take our mate off the hook and make him or her less responsible for the creation and maintenance of our happiness, an emotional release can occur within us. Our mate is no longer the villain, no longer the tormentor who set out to make us miserable. We can again see our mate as the friend we once knew.

In our work with couples, we have found that love is quite durable. Becoming actively responsible for happiness in our relationship allows us to rediscover early positive feelings and let go of the disappointments that evolved later in the marriage. When we all remember it is up to us to create the meaning and quality of our experience, we abandon condemnation, blame, and complaint, which allows us to relate once again as lovers as well as friends.

CHAPTER FOUR

Affairs: Falling into Temptation

*W*e all have visions of a perfect love and marriage in which we never hurt each other, always overlook each other's flaws, and are honest and open, supportive and accepting. We rejoice in our spouse's triumphs and close ranks during the hard times, we are loyal and trustworthy, and although we make mistakes we also care enough to forgive. But above all, we are faithful. As the Bible commands, we will not commit adultery.

How is it possible then for husbands and wives to shed such honorable commitments and fall prey to temptation? And in ever-increasing numbers? Recent surveys have consistently placed fidelity at or very near the top of the list of marital values for both men and women. But curiously, infidelity has continued to rise. Back in the early 1950s, Kinsey found roughly half of all married men and a quarter of all married women had had at least one extramarital affair by the age of 40. Studies in the 1980s indicate a somewhat higher figure for men and a sharply higher figure for women. The Pill and the ensuing sexual revolution seem to have evened out the numbers, erasing any significant differences between men and women in terms of infidelity. How can we value fidelity so highly, fear betrayal so greatly, and still, in two out of every three marriages, indulge in extramarital affairs?

We believe affairs are always psychologically harmful for both instigator and spouse. Understanding how and why affairs come about is the first preventive measure a husband or wife can take to avert future affairs or deal with an existing one.

WHY AFFAIRS?

From our work with troubled couples, we are convinced that affairs today reflect attempts on the part of men and women to realize and satisfy, consciously or unconsciously, all those impossible expectations that are missing or thwarted in the marriage. Affairs are perhaps the most self-defeating manifestation of an Other-Directed marriage. They are foolish attempts to find external solutions to what are internal concerns—problems of self-worth and self-respect. It is as though the one who strays decides, "If I can't find what I so desperately want in my marriage, I'll look elsewhere—but I refuse to give up my wishes and fantasies."

One train of thought goes something like this: "I love you and want to make our marriage work. But something's wrong. I'm hurt, I'm angry, and nothing I can see is going to change. If you loved me as much as I thought you did, I wouldn't be feeling this way. What can I do? I've tried talking, explaining, and 'if you'll do this, I'll do that.' How am I going to get what I need? I don't think I necessarily want to leave, but . . . maybe someone else could help make me happy."

Wives and husbands have affairs when they reach a point where they see no hope of change in the relationship. While some individuals cope with such an impasse by becoming depressed or silently resigned, others seek external solutions to marital dilemmas. Disenchantment causes them to lose faith in the promise that marriage might satisfy those needs.

There are also individuals who may succumb to seduction even though they consciously feel relatively immune to such temptations. Anyone who uses denial as a way of dealing with unhappiness will eventually find out that life often intrudes in shocking ways. A husband or wife could be so well insulated emotionally from his or her own dissatisfactions that vulnerability or receptivity to an affair comes totally by surprise. "I never realized how deprived I felt" is an acknowledgment every therapist has heard hundreds of times.

Experimenting with a different partner or even scuttling the old one and finding a new one has been tacitly sanctioned by our society in recent years. During the 1970s, we saw affairs on the upswing and divorce statistics reach unprecedented heights. Rather than raising eyebrows, affairs and divorces were often seen as a proof of daring, courage, and appetite for adventure. It became fashionable to regard sexual experimentation as not particularly harmful and positively growth-enhancing, regardless of its impact on traditional relationships. But this is certainly not the way most people think today. In a recent poll in California, married people listed the qualities they felt were most important in husbands and wives, and number one on the list was fidelity! Certainly this is due in part to fear of AIDS, but it may also reflect an increasing desire for a solid marriage and a commitment to traditional values.

KINDS OF AFFAIRS

Affairs are then attempts to meet important needs that are unmet within the context of the marriage. The nature of these needs determines the person who will be sought out (or the person whom we will allow to seek us out), the length and depth of the affair, and even whether or not the affair will be disclosed to the spouse in one way or another.

The Need for Sexual Conquest

Men have always used sexual conquest as a way to measure power and attraction. In the past, women weren't supposed to enjoy sex all that much, and so a man's conquest really counted—he had overcome the obstacles, broken down the resistance, and she even enjoyed it! The sexual revolution changed all that. When it turned out that women not only enjoyed sex as much as men but felt entitled to be treated sensitively and equally in that area, the fun of sexual conquest was gone. When conquest came easily, it lost its appeal, for at the very heart of sexual conquest is challenge.

In the context of marriage, sexual conquest for men and women is but a distant memory. Yet many husbands and wives still harbor a secret wish for a particular kind of sexual excitement in marriage, something reminiscent of conquest—which is obviously an impossibility. Marriage can validate one's attractiveness or value as a person in a general way, but the kind of ecstatic validation that novelty and conquest can provide is something one only gets outside, by having an affair.

"I played around a lot when I was single," Bart relates with a sigh, "and I really thought I had it out of my system when I married Jan. I was completely faithful for six years. We had two kids, and between them and work, I didn't have the time or the energy even to think about anything else. But lately, I've been feeling bored at work and kind of detached at home, and I've found myself involved in a couple of flings." By "flings" Bart means affairs. He uses that term to communicate that his "flings" aren't important and that they pose no real threat to his marriage. Bart is wrong on both counts.

Bart doesn't have a bad marriage, and he is foolishly jeopardizing it by his deception and unfaithful behavior. He and Jan both work, both are frequently tired, and both have unfortunately let their relationship slip quietly into the background—everything else always comes first. They are both responsible for neglecting their love life; there is no clear villain or victim in this situation.

But the truth is that Bart is not simply bored at work, he is feeling ineffective and fearful that any chance for significant upward mobility has somehow eluded him. He doesn't feel challenged at work nor courageous enough to make changes in his career situation. These factors have had a serious and negative effect upon his feelings of confidence. Rather than allowing himself to be closer to Jan, and to be bolstered by the stability of their marriage, he looks outside to an affair. That choice seems easier and more predictably successful than facing the source of his frustrations—a career in which he feels ineffective.

Bart's need to lie and cover his tracks creates

a painful tension in their marriage that Jan senses even though she cannot as yet correctly identify the problem. In time, usually not too long, the instability at home and at work will create enough pressure that he will be forced to deal with both—let us hope in a positive fashion.

Sexual conquest for women is a relatively new phenomenon. Women have long been envious of men's ability to go aggressively after what they want. In recent years women have become much more sexually assertive and comfortable with initiation, but this new behavior has not always been well received by the man. This isn't to deny that many men have had a problem in this area that needs to be solved, for they do. But in the context of an important relationship, unfortunately the problem of one partner becomes the problem of both.

For years, Beth felt resigned to the fact that she could be assertive anywhere but in the bedroom. While she never really discussed this issue with her husband, she sensed his discomfort and secretly protected him from having to deal with it. As Beth explained, "I tried initiating sex with Bob a couple of times, but absolutely nothing happened. I mean, he couldn't get it up. He never said it but I knew what the problem was: he wanted me to be wildly responsive to his overtures, but he wasn't comfortable with my starting anything myself."

Frustrated with what felt like an unfair deal, Beth had three very short-term affairs during the last year. "It's hard for me to be passive,"

Beth continues. "I needed to feel I could have an impact on a man. It was exciting to be able to actively turn a man on." Beth found a way to reduce some of the sexual tensions and inequalities in her marriage by going outside the relationship. The problem was not just that Beth was not solving the dilemma in the context of her marriage, which is where the dilemma existed. Beth was really playing out an unconscious belief that when two people are in love, sex should be easy, lively, and never complicated by a mate's insecurities or conflicts. Of course, she was wrong.

After some months of extramarital activity, Beth found the courage to confront her husband with what she really had been feeling, being careful, of course, not to reveal her affair. Resistant at first, Bob gradually heard the new sense of resolve in her voice and agreed to go into marital counseling to discuss it further. He continued with the counselor on his own, learning to relax and become more comfortable with and accepting of his wife's sexual advances. His commitment to change was all Beth needed to become faithful again.

The Need for a Younger Lover

"Approaching 50 has been a lot harder than I thought it would be," Ken said pensively. "It seems like only yesterday that cops looked old to me, and now they look like kids. Women who smile and say hello to me are my wife's age, but the ones I find myself attracted to are all younger. It's disconcerting when you realize women are talking to you not because they find you interesting but because they think you're safe."

We live in a youth-oriented culture. Young is virile, attractive, and sexy; old is not. As we grow older, we must cope with vanishing youth. During this process, many of us stop feeling attractive and valued as a lover. Where once we might have felt irresistible, even powerful, now we begin to feel the cooling of our mate's sexual fires. All of this, of course, is quite natural. But when you mix together the gradual waning of sexual passions, aging, insecurities, and needs for validation that are not being fulfilled at home, then you have the makings of a potential affair. In most marriages, none of these factors taken alone is significant, but if they all come together, one spouse is likely to seek a younger lover.

Jane, 44, is a strong, powerful, and successful lawyer. She has been married for eighteen years to a man who has always loved her but who over the years has become rather complacent, probably a little dull, and certainly not as vital or as attentive to her as he once was. The frequency and intensity of their sexual contact has diminished over the last several years because of performance concerns on his part. They love each other, but Jane's need to feel desirable remains unsatisfied.

Recently at a retreat held by her law firm she spent a great deal of time during drinks and dinner talking and dancing with a younger associate, Ted. Jane's unspoken wish had been answered. "I realized then what was missing in my life. I was getting to be an old lady. My mind was being validated through my work, my value as a wife and mother was confirmed at home, but my needs as a woman were being neglected."

Two weeks later, Jane began her affair with Ted. Since then she has spent a number of afternoons with him, and on two occasions a weekend away while she was taking depositions out of town. Jane goes on to say, "In the beginning it was wonderful. I can't remember the last time I felt so alive. It wasn't that the sex was all that great, because he wasn't any more expert a lover than Bill is, but I felt wonderful. I felt as if a kind of dreary gray cloud over my life had been lifted. But now I'm beginning to get concerned because I can see him looking at other women, women who are all conspicuously younger than I am. I feel awful these days more often than I feel good. Bill thinks it's that I'm under a lot of pressure at work, so I end up feeling horribly guilty."

Basically Jane's problem centers around her fears of aging, of diminishing youth, of losing her attractiveness. We all need to learn to come to terms with the changes that occur in our lives, and aging is one of them. We can't avoid growing older, so denying it, which is essentially what Jane attempted to do, is not constructive. At the present time, her husband, Bill, doesn't know that Jane is having an affair, but he certainly knows that something is going on. She dresses differently, she's less available to him, and, perhaps most important, she is more irritable with him, because she is feeling guilty about the affair and also because she's living a life of deception.

Affairs such as Jane's usually go undetected, and they most often end as quickly as they begin. She will not be able to tolerate the level of dishonesty she feels, and her caring for Bill is strong enough to bring her back into a bond with him.

When a man has an affair with a younger woman, the central dynamic is also typically one of power and renewed sexuality. Even in good marriages, men sometimes have feelings of lost strength and vitality. If wanting to feel desirable and attractive drives women to seek a younger lover, it is wanting to feel effective and have an impact that pushes men in that same direction. Men who, after a certain age, do not feel particularly successful at work are especially vulnerable to self-doubts about their strength and competence. At home this man frequently feels taken for granted, and at work he feels disappointed and overshadowed by others' successes. He may look at his wife of a similar age as undeniable proof that he too is getting older. His wife may be strong, warm, and loving toward him, but he may crave a kind of adoration from her that is impossible—and inappropriate— for her to give him.

Wayne is 46, balding and a few pounds overweight, none of which in any way bothers his wife. In fact, Carol has made it very clear to him that she finds men who are balding very sexy and attractive. Rather than making Wayne feel better, her reassurances have actually had the opposite effect and annoy him. He has been contemplating getting hair plugs, and Carol makes him feel silly and superficial for wanting to look younger. Carol, who is a year older, is very accepting of the passage of time. She is not at all interested in the rather strenuous aerobic exercises that Wayne keeps trying to talk her into. She no longer has the firm body of a younger woman, but that is just fine with her. It is not fine with Wayne. His unconscious expectation is that they should both remain youthful and vital always, regardless of their age.

These frustrations eventually propelled Wayne into the quest for a younger woman. He met Michelle, who is fifteen years younger, and initiated a stormy affair, which, like so many, was exciting in the beginning. Later, it became guilt-inducing, as the lying and evenings of deception began to weigh heavily on him. His increasing guilt and his anger at Carol for not being Michelle escalated to the point where they sought marital counseling. Carol never found out about the affair, and Wayne is still trying to sort out his values and grapple with aging in a way that will not permanently damage his marriage.

Wayne is a victim of his own unrealistic expectations about marriage. We cannot expect our marriage partners to keep us young, help us deny the passage of time and its effects upon us, or assume responsibility for our insecurities about getting older.

The Need to Overcome Depression

Depression can be an incredibly complex phenomenon. It affects far more people than we realize and can appear under a number of different disguises: as fatigue, illness, even a sleep or eating disorder. Men and women are equally susceptible to depression, although it may be more hidden in men because they are accustomed to denying important but bothersome feelings.

Frequently, the conscious experience of depression is boredom, a lack of any real excitement, and a vague feeling that life is passing us by. But depression isn't really related to these feelings at all. Depression is a by-product of helplessness and unexpressed anger about not feeling fulfilled. When we are fulfilled at work we feel actively engaged and acknowledged, and we have a sense of worth. When we are emotionally fulfilled, we feel the same way. When we have lost a feeling of connectedness to either work or a mate, there is a high probability of sinking slowly into a state of chronic sadness.

Whatever the real source of sadness, marriage partners are often blamed. If something is wrong, it must be "their" fault. If we're not happy, "they" are responsible, and if we're lonely and down, it must be because of "them." These feelings lead to the expectation that our mate should somehow be able to make us happier and to help us feel more alive.

The antidote for so many of us when we feel sad is to look for something that will give us a "high," something that will stimulate us. Men and women tend to view excitement a bit differently. For men, excitement is most frequently attached to work, while for women it is associated with relationships. When it comes to feeling vaguely depressed, men are susceptible to having affairs to create the excitement they don't find in their jobs. Women are vulnerable to having affairs to stir up the excitement they miss or cannot sustain in their relationships. Both reasons for affairs are foolish, destructive, and preventable. There are many ways to feel excited. We must all learn to discover sources of passion and excitement in life without hurting relationships we need and cherish.

The Need to Avoid Dependency

If there is one benefit we should expect from a marriage, it is the ability to depend on our mate. Indeed, for many husbands and wives, leaning on each other, feeling the other person is there, is the strongest connection in marriage. In a sound marriage, trusting that you can share your innermost thoughts and concerns is what makes husbands and wives feel loved and loving.

Sometimes a spouse says, "I'm not sure whether you love me or whether you just need me," and, in fact, dependency is such an integral part of the marriage bond that it is almost impossible to separate it out. But there is a kind of affair that takes place which is a direct result of fear of this dependency. Some husbands and wives will not allow themselves to become too needful of their mate and therefore find themselves looking for satisfaction outside the marriage. They may not be conscious of this inner dynamic, but they engage in a kind of "splitting" by which certain functions are relegated to the spouse and others, left unsatisfied, are then sought in the world outside the marriage.

Jerry loves his wife, has been married for twenty-three years, has three kids, and has no intention of ever leaving his home. But something is missing from his marriage. In the early years, when he was essentially a workaholic, he felt his marriage was fine. Home was a refuge, and his buddies were his confidants regarding work. As years went on and he became more established in his law practice, he felt less driven and more confident. But with the passage of time, he also craved a deeper kind of communication and intimacy. Jerry wanted to feel close to a woman and able to open up about getting older, exploring life's meaning, and other concerns. He felt he couldn't do this with his wife. Not because she wasn't available to him, for indeed she was. But so much time had gone by, he didn't have any idea how he could become more intimate with her. And he didn't even try.

A spouse's changing and maturing needs for deeper contact and intimacy can arouse a great deal of anxiety. Jerry and his wife are not used to sharing these feelings. To become more open and to express hidden feelings of uncertainty was hard for Jerry to do. As he told us, "I've known for a long time that I wanted something richer, but it's just never been part of how we are together. We talk about money, the kids, friends, and that kind of thing, but not much about feelings." So all of a sudden something different seemed scary.

Jerry was primed for an affair. Dependency needs, as pent up as his had become, desperately seek some expression. He found Erica, a woman who worked in his company, and their after-work drinks became dinner dates, and before long, Jerry was going over to her apartment. He found in Erica the willingness to listen warmly, caringly, and without judgment. He insisted to his best friend that he couldn't have this kind of communication with his wife, but he was wrong. His expectations about marriage, instead of being exaggerated, were actually too diminished. After some months, he broke off the affair and sought counseling. In time he discovered his wife had similar longings for a closer relationship, but she too was unable to set them in motion.

There are many couples like this today, emotionally hungry, but unable to believe there is any hope of satisfying their need with their spouse. For these people, allowing themselves to rely on a mate is dangerous, tantamount to putting all their eggs in one basket. They can't conceive of doing this, so they don't even try. For them, a husband or wife plays a particular role in their life: provider, mother or father of their children. They feel good about being married, but the bond is not as deep or broad for them as it can be, and as it is for others who have richer and fuller marriages because they impose no artificial constraints.

The most common reason men and women sometimes see their spouse in a fragmented form comes from their observing a similar kind of relationship when they grew up. Boys may have seen fathers treat wives as mothers and housekeepers rather than lovers and confidantes. Girls may have grown up seeing their mothers talk about Dad as a rather important yet emotionally distant provider and protector of the household. In either case, they have been raised with the idea that husbands and wives play out roles that are specific, defined, and rigid, allowing no room for the full marriage experience that we all want and need.

Given the fact that women generally have an easier time with emotions and dependency, one

would think that women would be less susceptible to this kind of affair. Nothing could be
further from the truth. As psychologists we have
seen an enormous rise in the number of women
who, in effect, refuse to allow a normal dependency to occur with their husbands and who
have one affair after another over a period of
years. It's almost as though they must have a
"backup" in addition to their husband. Consciously they may tell themselves they're looking for romance and sexual excitement, but these
women will often acknowledge that their husband may even be much more satisfying sexually than their secret lover! Yet the affairs go on.
In fact, between affairs such women feel very
anxious, for they sense they are becoming too
dependent on their husband.

Ellen had had five serious affairs in her nine-
teen years of marriage. She described her husband as nice, loving, a good father, and . . .
boring. Their friends didn't see him as boring at
all, but she insisted there was something missing. What was in fact absent was a stronger
bond of intimacy that Ellen would not allow to
take place with her husband. In therapy, Ellen
described a very painful first love affair in college that ended when she discovered her boyfriend was secretly seeing another girl. Crushed,
bitter, and forever wary, Ellen unconsciously
made a vow never to be hurt in that way again.
From that time on, every relationship with a
man had been incomplete because she split off
a part of her soul from the relationship. Her

wish for closeness and intimacy was met by having lovers on the side. "I was a fool ever to trust a man," she said, defending her serial infidelity. Ellen, as so many of us do in lesser ways, was allowing an old experience to forever distort the ways in which she viewed men, love, and relationships. Even after thirteen years of marriage, she refused to allow the reality of her husband's essential trustworthiness to penetrate her defensive shell. In time, after many months of therapy, Ellen gradually let down her guard and began to reveal more feelings to her husband, thus healing past scars with present love.

Interestingly, when affairs based on blocked dependency evolve into actual talk of divorce and a marriage between the lovers, something happens. It is then that the dependency between the spouses which has been denied and dormant will emerge, often in powerful ways. How often have you seen people who are determined to leave the marriage and may even move out briefly and then are suddenly shocked to find out just how dependent they have become in spite of themselves! Their dependency, however, is not a healthy dependency but rather an ambivalent one based on both loving and hateful feelings.

This type of affair is a good proof of the fact that men and women are basically designed to have full, nonfragmented relationships with each other. When a critical need such as dependency is split off and forced out of the marriage, then there is no recourse but to gratify those needs elsewhere. This is sad when, in fact, the proper place for the satisfaction of those needs is at home!

The Need to Find Satisfaction Elsewhere

Perhaps the most common reason people give for having an affair is a variation of "I had to get what was missing at home." As we just noted, often what is missing is something a spouse will actually not permit in the marriage.

Many of us are derelict when it comes to letting our mate know directly what it is we need and how important it is that we get it. This often happens because people themselves don't realize how significant these needs are and how serious the consequences may be to the marriage if they go unmet. Most often, we drift into affairs rather than plan them. Frequently, the discovery of what's missing isn't made until the person finds it in his or her feelings for another person.

We probably all want far too much in our marriage. We expect it to be a kind of magical union that promises and delivers a steady and uncomplicated output of satisfying experiences. Even though our sophisticated intellect tells us otherwise, we hope our marriage will somehow beat the odds and remain unflawed. And we are let down and disappointed when it fails to achieve that impossible standard. When we in-

tentionally look beyond the marriage for fulfillment, the type of infidelity that results is often
the most destructive to the relationship, since
the wish for an affair and the subsequent anger
and resentment toward one's spouse are so
conscious.

Richard, age 49, has been complaining about
his wife's lack of sexual interest for years. No
amount of therapy or cajoling has had an effect.
He finds himself frequently drifting into liaisons, usually on business trips. He feels no
guilt and in fact feels rather self-righteous about
what he does.

Richard's wife, Cara, knows about some of
his affairs and suspects others. "It got pretty
tense the other day," Richard explains, "when
a hotel mailed an earring to my house thinking
that it belonged to my wife. I found myself
spinning out some story about it being a stupid
mistake, but I know it sounded lame. I guess
the truth is that it didn't bother me all that
much that she suspected. I don't want her to
think that what goes on at home is acceptable."

The problem with Richard and Cara is that
they are unfortunately involved in a vicious circle. A good deal of Cara's sexual disinterest
isn't real disinterest at all, but hurt and angry
withholding. She isn't willing to let down her
guard and open herself intimately and affec-
tionately because she is aware of his easy wan-
derings. She blames the "problem" on issues of
trust and consistency, while Richard justifies
his affairs as reasonable solutions to the gaps in

their relationship. Neither of them is willing to do anything different, which is the only hope of changing things, so the cold war goes on.

Annette, age 39, was one of those women, numerous today, who find their husbands suffer too many "headaches." This is the classic problem of inhibited sexual desire on the part of the man. Her husband, Rex, said he was overworked, hassled by financial anxieties, and frankly not as interested in sex as he once was. In the course of therapy, it was revealed that his disinterest in sex coincided with Annette's having taken a course in human sexuality at the local college. She believed that Rex became too lazy or threatened when she finally told him he was not engaging in enough foreplay to satisfy her.

Rex was not nearly so disinterested as he was anxious and uncomfortable. He wasn't used to viewing their sexual encounters as "lovemaking," and the growing feeling that he was somehow responsible for Annette's sexual fulfillment made him feel his sexual behavior was being scrutinized and graded. Rather than extending himself, doing something new, and taking a few chances, Rex solved the whole problem by pretty much avoiding sex altogether. It was only after Annette threatened to look elsewhere for sexual fulfillment that Rex was shocked into examining his unspoken concerns about his sexual prowess and how these concerns were interfering with an important aspect of their relationship. It was fortunate for them both that

Annette was so honest and direct, for it allowed them to deal more constructively with their problems than if she had actually initiated an affair.

Lonnie has a different sort of problem. At 56, she feels her long marriage with Jeffrey has become silent and solitary now that the children are grown and on their own. Rather than trying to discover some new interests or activities they might both enjoy, they haven't altered their life-style at all—he still focuses on his furniture business and she on raising horses. A few months ago, Lonnie met a man at a horse show with whom she immediately felt comfortable. Over the last several weeks she has seen him a number of times for lunch or just to talk. "I can't tell you how much I enjoy him," she exclaims. "We're interested in all the same things. I feel as if I could talk to him for hours and, I think, still want more. We haven't done anything physical, even though the thought has occurred to me, and I certainly haven't told Jeff about him!"

Lonnie is playing with an explosive situation, and if she continues, an affair will surely develop. Rather than simply observing the lack of shared experiences at home, Lonnie needs to expend some energy to create such experiences. She is rapidly drifting away from her husband, and the only way to alter the situation is for her to sit down with him and develop a joint plan to start exploring new ways of being together.

When problems within a marriage are consciously solved by affairs outside, the net effect is overwhelmingly negative. The person engaging in the affair often wishes that he or she did not have to do it. The person may wish that instead of being in some hotel during the afternoon, he or she were back at work or at home. The necessary deception involved makes unfaithful spouses even angrier at their mate than they were before the affair began. These vague resentments are invariably brought back into the marriage and crop up in many different ways, which we will explore later. Suffice it to say that even though the unfaithful ones have convinced themselves that they are justified, that very sense of self-righteousness brings up even more resentment.

The Need for Novel Sexual Contact

Often in psychotherapy we will see a patient who married at a relatively young age, never really had a variety of romantic experiences as an adult, and now feels deprived of those adventures. These individuals believe they have missed out on some very special moments. They are happily married, perhaps, yet constantly bombarded by ads, stories, and movies about the most exciting and erotic experiences imaginable: the stranger who suddenly enters your life whom you feel you've known forever, or the person you've secretly desired from afar who now recognizes and wants you. You love your spouse, and yet . . . are you going to live the rest of your life without tasting these intense moments? When a man or woman marries without ever having had a previous sexual experience, the secret curiosity can be overwhelming.

Husbands and wives who have had a limited or nonexistent history of love affairs prior to marriage are primed for affairs whose primary lure is novelty and the excitement of the forbidden unknown. This is especially true of those women who do not have careers and are not working at something that continues to arouse their excitement and passion.

As psychologists, we often feel in a quandary, for these desires are not easily dismissed as "neurotic." Indeed, if we assume that the quest for adventure is healthy, even desirable, then what's the matter with sexual adventures? The answer is not a simple one. Often our best response is to advise the patient to consider the downside, the risk to the marriage, and to struggle with the notion that we all must give up certain wishes or fantasies when they conflict with other more valued aspects of life.

Gayle, 33, has been married ten years, has two small children, and gave up her job when the children came along. She finds herself very busy at home and is also involved in a few activities outside. While reasonably happy at home, Gayle is and always has been a romantic, much to the exhaustion of her husband. He sees her as never having enough excitement in life. He gets home tired, and she's ready to go out, anywhere. They understand their differences, and it's usually not the source of any serious conflict. But Gayle has harbored fantasies of an affair for the last few years. She has married women friends who have done so, and even though the affairs ultimately ended painfully, Gayle still envies their daring and secret adventures.

She chose to have a brief affair with Andrew, a man eight years younger than she, whom she met at her health club. The first two encounters were, according to her, ecstatic, everything she hoped they would be. She stopped seeing Andrew after the second week, primarily because of her fear of being discovered. She doesn't regret what she did, and yet when she is truly honest with herself she is unsure of the benefits. "It was like being a drug addict for two weeks. I was high all the time, and yet I knew this couldn't be a steady diet for me—I knew things would suffer at home."

The analogy of drugs and addiction is a common one for both men and women, who ask themselves whether something that feels so good can be bad for you. Frankly, the answer is yes. Just as there seems to be no drug that, with continued use, doesn't begin to have serious side effects, so too with affairs. Eventually you pay. In time, some other part of the system begins to malfunction. There are no perfect escapist drugs, and there is no perfect and ultimately harmless affair.

The Need for a Double Life

We have all heard of affairs going on for years. The great romance of Spencer Tracy and Katharine Hepburn comes to mind. Rather than calling such an arrangement an "affair," it is much more accurate to characterize the participants as having a "double life." These involvements typically arise from a marriage that has strong ties holding it together. We're not suggesting that the ties are necessarily positive ones, but they are binding. For some, these ties are religious. For others, there may be a seriously ill husband or wife who cannot be abandoned. And, more commonly, there are those marriages in which the family life is so rich and meaningful that neither the husband nor the wife can contemplate leaving the marriage, at least until the children are grown. Even after the children leave, people often remain together "for the children's sake" or because they are afraid of their friends' response if they decide to dissolve the marriage.

In many ways, this type of affair, if unknown to the spouse, may represent the most deceptive and hypocritical relationship of all. Try to picture yourself with another wife or husband you see two or three times a week. And this goes on for years. How do you do it? How can you share your thoughts about your children, your work, and so on, when you have to do the same thing at home? Well, it's obvious what happens: sharing of feelings and thoughts with the mate at home becomes superficial or even nonexistent, as though that person were merely a symbolic figure with whom you may, for example, share some family concerns but rarely deeper, more personal revelations. Real joy and passions are taking place elsewhere.

Men and women who are inclined to have this sort of dual relationship always feel resigned to not finding closeness and intensity within their marriages. Most often, they haven't really looked all that hard at home or put out all that much effort. They assume the path toward passion and aliveness within the marriage is too overgrown. In fact, they simply choose the easier road.

Betty, age 47, has had an ongoing affair with her gynecologist for nine years. Neither has any intention of leaving his or her marriage, although the fantasy of what it would be like to be together more openly fuels many of their erotic afternoons. Each of them would never dream of having another affair; they consider themselves "soul mates" and fortunate to have met. Betty's husband is a reasonably successful aerospace engineer, though hardly the most stimulating or emotionally expressive of men. Eric, the gynecologist, is married to a woman who is forever absorbed in one social activity or another. Eric loves her, but finds it difficult to regard her as a sexual being. He admits to Betty that he has sex with her once or twice a month just to keep up a semblance of normal marital relations. Betty, on the other hand, has a much more active sex life with her husband but finds other aspects of their marriage deficient. Even though she loves him, she finds they have grown apart with respect to intellectual interests, an area that forms a central core of her bond with Eric.

What can we make of this type of arrangement? Is it bad? Will it last? Does it matter? The only certainty is that the ongoing deception has a continuing impact on both marriages. Naturally, any wish or commitment to make changes at home has long since passed. They are both satisfied, they believe they have the best of both worlds, and they insist they are not hurting their spouses. As happens in most long-term affairs, companionship rather than sexuality has become the strongest bonding element between Eric and Betty. In fact, many times in their liaisons, they will just talk rather than have any sexual contact.

In some ways, the double-life affair is similar to arrangements that have always existed in certain European cultures. However, Betty and Eric refer to each other as special "friends" rather than "lover" or "mistress." It should be noted that while they say they are happy, they both express sadness that things couldn't have been different with their mates. Keeping such an important part of their lives hidden for so long creates a vague sense of fragmentation that becomes the source of inner doubting. Though both Eric and Betty seem to be juggling their double lives fairly well, one always wonders what might have been if they had had the courage to work harder on their marriages.

The Need for Revenge

Feeling wronged, betrayed, "cuckolded," can lead to an affair whose sole purpose is revenge. We all know what the desire for revenge feels like, though most of us don't put our "an eye for an eye" feelings into action. For instance, when our spouse appears to be flirting at a party, our anger and discomfort can lead us to want to do the very same thing, to let the other person know how hurt we are or even how tenuous the relationship could become if the flirting were to continue.

Jealousy is one of the most powerful and potentially destructive of all human emotions. And the wish to strike back, to retaliate in kind, is an all too common response. If a husband or wife is cursed with an overly active imagination, it doesn't take long before a flirtation is perceived as a possible infidelity. We can all be a little paranoid; it's easy to conjure up a worst-case scenario. Usually, though, coolness and maturity prevail, and we can keep our fears in check rather than doing something rash.

There are situations, however, that do give rise to rage and a thirst for revenge even in the most healthy of us. When men and women discover their mate has had or is having an affair, it is one of the most crushing of life's experiences. A common response is the wish to pay the mate back, to make him or her feel the same hurt. First you feel as though you want to die, then you think that maybe your mate should. Often the revenge affair is conducted in a way that is guaranteed to be detected.

Melanie, age 27, found out her husband had had an affair while away at a weekend conference. She was told by the wife of another man at the conference, although the reasons why she was told are suspect. So often such disclosures are couched in the language of friendship when in fact they are really just gossip of an extremely destructive nature. Melanie's friend said she thought she was doing Melanie a favor by letting her know. Melanie confronted her husband, Dave, who vehemently, but not very convincingly, denied the affair. Melanie was certain she had been betrayed and immediately began plotting her revenge. She called up an old boyfriend who was still single, met him at a bar, and went to a motel with him. Subtlety and finesse are not Melanie's strong points, and that very evening she blurted out the whole experience to Dave, who became enraged, grabbed a few items of clothing, and left the house.

Dave and Melanie did manage to patch up things, spent a few sessions with a counselor, and pledged anew their fidelity to each other. While unfortunate, this kind of crisis in a marriage can often be solved quite readily. It was an isolated event, we presume, and a certain Biblical kind of justice, an eye for an eye, took place without any lasting damage to the marriage. But there are revenge affairs that are far more destructive.

Particularly harmful to a marriage is the revenge affair that involves the best friend of one of the spouses. This happens more often than one would like to think. The parties to this affair will often insist that it was pure happenstance, that the affair came out of familiarity, closeness, and friendship that had existed over time. In our view, many of these affairs are in fact motivated by an unconscious wish to avenge some hurt. We believe this because to have an affair with your spouse's best friend is such an extreme act of duplicity and betrayal that it has to be motivated by something more than lust and physical proximity.

Some retaliatory affairs are motivated not by the other person's infidelity, but by a profound sense of neglect on the part of a husband or wife. But unlike those affairs that come about from a sense of deprivation at home and a wish to find what's missing elsewhere, these affairs are pure acts of anger. Men and women involved in such an affair will actually be thinking, while in the throes of lovemaking, how much this would hurt their spouse if the spouse knew. Their rage is mixed with self-righteousness, but there is little if any real pleasure involved.

Using infidelity as a way of getting back at a spouse and evening up the score is seldom really satisfying. And it is potentially more harmful to the vengeance seeker than the actual "crime" was. Revenge is fundamentally a denial of the imperfection of human beings and their union—marriage. It may be a potent form of punishment for a partner having broken the promise of faith, but it cannot solve the real problem in the marriage.

HOW AFFAIRS AFFECT MARRIAGE

Let us state at the outset that affairs are terribly destructive not only to marriages but to the individuals involved as well.

The most basic effect of an affair on one's marriage is estrangement. Some people think a lack of trust is the ultimate legacy, but that assumes that the affair becomes known. The fact is that most affairs go undetected. Most husbands and wives will never really know for sure whether their loved one has been faithful or not.

Affairs are inherently dishonest; they all involve varying degrees of subterfuge and deception. Maintaining the "secret" requires a tremendous amount of energy even if the unfaithful party doesn't think so. We have spoken with and counseled many men and women having affairs who at first insist they are carrying it off well. They report little or no guilt and are convinced the affair does not negatively affect their relationship at home. This is absolute nonsense!

In order to keep an affair hidden you are forever walking around with a secret that burns inside. Imagine having a liaison, then coming home, making love with your spouse, and at the height of lovemaking saying, "I love you." Pretty hard to do, isn't it? Yet millions of men and women have experienced that very moment. What must that do to a person's sense of honor, integrity, character?

As for those who insist they feel little or no guilt, they are deceiving themselves. Guilt is not always conscious. Husbands or wives who play around may feel hidden guilt, which manifests itself in irritability, argumentativeness with one's spouse, or vague and ill-defined feelings of depression and self-loathing. Sometimes this unconscious guilt is linked to a secret wish to be caught—so it will all be over and the burden will be lifted. Perhaps it seems contradictory to speak of affairs as providing both excitement and a sense of heavy burden—but usually they do. There is often so much juggling of work life, home life, and the affair that ending it can be a relief rather than a time of sadness. We have listened to men and women joke about how good it feels to stay home with the family rather than having to conjure up ever more elaborate excuses to explain their working late or chronic absences.

The expression "Adultery is for adults" conveys the notion that it takes a certain kind of caring and maturity in order to carry off an affair successfully. Many people cannot handle the inner burden of lies and deception, so one day they blurt out the truth. As with any wrong-doing there is always a concomitant need to confess. Some people will simply tell the truth, while others will unconsciously set up a situation that will expose them. The effect on one's spouse is the same regardless: shock, intense pain, rage, and doubt that this hurt can ever heal and trust be reestablished.

As a rule of thumb, we never advocate confessions, for the harm they may do is all too often irreparable. People who confess do it for selfish reasons. They are not thinking of their mate; instead, their only wish is to relieve themselves of the horrible secret and expiate their guilt.

LIFE AFTER THE AFFAIR

Can there ever be a feeling of trust between husband and wife after such disclosures? We believe it is possible, but only when there is also a heightened attention to whatever may have been missing in the marriage that precipitated the breach. People today are generally more forgiving about infidelities than in the past, but the wound and the inevitable distrust heal slowly. The "tincture of time" does work, but it must be accompanied by even greater amounts of love and reassurance than before. By love, we mean actions, not repeated apologies or empty promises. One must be willing to give greater amounts of affection and do many more unselfish deeds and thoughtful acts of kindness. The adulterer often feels as though he or she is on trial—and it is a trial! But the sentence can end with the right attitude. Healing typically takes more time than one hopes, but less time than one fears.

A word of caution. In a marriage that is recovering from an affair, typically the "guilty" one and the "injured" party are on emotionally different timetables. The one who has committed the affair hopes, even sincerely believes, the pain is in the past. Consequently, he or she is surprised and frustrated by, for example, the reluctance of the mate to resume sexual activity and other ways of feeling closer. It takes time, often many months, before trust can be reestablished. Expecting it too quickly can communicate to the "injured" one that there is still a lack of real caring and sensitivity.

It is all too convenient to blame our spouse, too easy to experience disappointment within the marriage and then look outside for apparent solutions. Affairs represent a clear shift in responsibility. When we are single, it is difficult to avoid taking responsibility for those aspects of our lives that are painful or unfulfilling. But when we marry, we can more easily duck that responsibility. Marriage becomes the ideal foil—we no longer have to look to ourselves as the source of satisfaction, because it is our mate's job to provide it. We are off the hook at last. It is precisely at that moment that we become vulnerable to having an affair. We couldn't create perfection within ourselves, we didn't find it in our marriage, so the search goes on. It doesn't dawn on us that our expectations are impossible. We blindly believe we can find the solution in the arms of another.

Throughout this book we emphasize how critical it is for each of us in a marriage to become as Self-Directed as possible, to find the source of power within us rather than looking to our mate as the catalyst. Having affairs will rob anyone of the inner integrity and self-esteem necessary for taking real control of one's life.

CHAPTER FIVE
When Lovers Fight

*P*eople fight, even in good marriages. Some couples become accustomed to fights, a few find solutions, but many husbands and wives are so inwardly horrified by their clashes they find neither relief nor resolution. Such individuals are mistakenly convinced that fights are bad and always incompatible with love. They are wrong. Couples can both fight and be in love with each other. Arguments, disputes, and heated exchanges are not inherently destructive, nor are they an indication that a marriage is headed toward dissolution. Indeed, most fighting is really an intense form of impassioned communication, a way of expressing the cumulative effects of long-standing and unresolved differences, frustrations, and resentments.

Couples who have a reflexive fear of fights, who shy away from disagreements, who cringe upon hearing the venting of intense emotions, are often the ones whose marriage can be in greater danger behind a veil of congeniality and seeming harmony.

However, our goal is certainly not to promote fighting but rather to illustrate ways to grapple with this issue.

Feeling paralyzed or blindly lashing back when attacked is falling prey to Other-Directedness in marriage just as is bullying your mate in order to get your way. Both kinds of behavior are indications of a belief that solutions to marital conflicts involve changing your mate. As counselors, we find that helping couples understand why fights occur and why they are so unnerving is far more important than trying to get them to learn how to act as their own referees. While learning to "fight fair" and "negotiate" sounds fine, such "skills" rarely work; fighting is just too threatening to many people. The Self-Directed person ponders rather than reacts; he or she asks what is really going on and attempts to come to grips with the real issues.

All relationships have areas of difference of opinion, and differences can be noisy if both parties are relatively free and honest with their feelings. Even though there is no other relationship as likely to achieve heightened states of love as a marriage, at the same time this very partnership can also elicit the most intense feelings of anger, hatred, and even violence. Marriage involves interdependencies and mutual needs, and threats to them can lead to enormous insecurity and retaliatory feelings. Fighting is a normal and inherent part of any bond that is so meaningful to the parties involved.

THE HUMAN DRAMA

Conflict provides the drama of life. Everyone loves a love story, but much of what we read and find compelling involves the darker side of relationships. Great literature is replete with tales of intense passions between men and women, unrequited or unconsummated love, and painful partings. What is often most fascinating is love gone awry. The reason we are drawn so magnetically to love's conflicts is that we all have secret fears of abandonment, betrayal, and disappointment, and reading about the torment of others is a way of confronting our terror.

From the turn of the century on, playwrights such as Ibsen, Chekhov, and Albee with his well-known play *Who's Afraid of Virginia Woolf?* have struggled to capture love's anguish. These writers focus on the intense emotions of men and women who are linked intimately and passionately by their fears as well as by their hopes and expectations. The tremendous impact of this kind of drama is due to the fact that it touches us in a very naked and powerful way. While all of us may not act out such primitive feelings as rage and jealousy, we all occasionally have such feelings.

Love and hate are, unfortunately, sometimes inextricably linked. Since this is so, it is incumbent on each of us to understand how to protect ourselves and our spouse from the hate—how to keep our fighting within the bounds of ethical and psychological sensitivity. Obviously the first step in this understanding is accepting the fact that fights do occur and that it doesn't automatically follow that the fighting couple should be considering a divorce. Fighting is unproductive, but most of the time it is not destructive enough to end the relationship.

Among the myths that plague marriages today is the belief that instability is intrinsically harmful in marriage. We know that to be false. In fact, there are many men and women whose differences cause not just fights but lively dialogues that are the very elements that sustain their passion for each other. If opposites attract, then couples who are drawn to each other because of these complementary traits must also take responsibility for the static caused by such polarities. Some couples are temperamentally suited to each other because of the passion they evoke in each other. The fear of acknowledging such antagonistic feelings can actually cause severe disruption between a husband and wife. What is better—to vent feelings, or to push them underground only for them to crop up in the form of disdain, indifference, and unspoken hostility? Instability is part of any marriage, and becoming more comfortable with it and with the intense emotions accompanying it is critical.

ARE LOVE AND HATE RELATED?

Beginning with Freud, psychoanalytic thinkers have explored the nature of love and hate and why these two seemingly contradictory emotional responses are linked. Essentially they have suggested that it has to do with unresolved childhood needs being carried forward into adult relationships. If we project onto our mate all of our fantasies and needs and demand that our spouse be everything to us, both parent and peer, then it follows that we are also likely to respond to our spouse in the same way we did to our parents. Instead of always being mature and accepting of reality, we respond in childlike and primitive ways at times. For example, disappointment may lead to irritability, anger, frustration, even tantrums. We end up wanting our loved one to be everything our parent wasn't —unconditionally caring, always there, always perfectly in tune with what we need. When this is not the reality, we respond with anger, rage, even vengeful fantasies. Of course, we would all like to think we have matured sufficiently that we no longer are driven by such primitive feelings. But none of us is completely cured of childhood pain, and so we still play out these old dramas.

The concept of ambivalence, the ability to both love and hate our marital partner, comes into play because of these very primitive thoughts. If we are dependent upon a spouse, and the spouse plays a pivotal role in validating our self-worth, then it follows that the spouse's power, even if it is only in our mind, will stimulate not only love, but anger related to the fear that this love will be withdrawn. At times, we may actually come to hate the very person we love—not necessarily at the same time, of course, but even that is possible.

Possessiveness is fueled by some of these darker aspects of love and desire. If we truly love our mate in a mature sense, we can let our mate be whoever he or she wants to be. But in addition to caring for our mate, we also need him or her. Our love is full and generous so long as our dependency is not threatened. Marital love is always to some degree conditional and interdependent, and that is where the trouble starts. To wish it were otherwise is totally unrealistic. When you make a commitment, when you want a person to be your lifelong companion, you are linking your happiness and emotional well-being to him or her. And if your mate does things that threaten that bond, you are likely to respond in the same way anyone does when the basic sense of security is shaken— with anxiety, anger, and even rage.

Perhaps the most important thing to realize about fights in marriage is that anger is typically a secondary response that serves as a cover for hurt feelings. Most people are not inherently mean or evil, but when they are angry they are responding to some real, imagined, or anticipated hurt. For most people, it is easier to get angry than it is to feel and express hurt feelings. Now, this doesn't mean you should automatically put up with angry outbursts. Nothing is sadder than to see women who are physically abused continue to excuse their husband's behavior because of the remorse he may exhibit after the deed: "He really didn't mean it. He broke down and apologized afterward." Understanding why someone is consciously cruel doesn't imply that we should tolerate it at any level.

The pairing of love and hate is familiar to many couples who find themselves fighting and then making up by engaging in sexual relations. Indeed, many couples are surprised at the intensity of passion in their lovemaking when it spontaneously follows a heated argument. The phenomenon illustrates how anger can block loving or even erotic feelings. When negative feelings are expressed in an argument, there is an emotional release, and the positive feelings begin to flow freely again.

EXPRESSIVENESS: A RELEASE OR A WEAPON?

When couples are in marriage therapy, one of the first things that happens is that the therapist elicits complaints and then asks, "Have you told that to your spouse?" This directive comes about for two reasons. The first is to see how well the husband and wife communicate with each other. The second reason is implicitly based on the theory that pent-up feelings or frustrations are not good and that ventilating them lets off steam, enabling the person to feel better.

Today, psychologists are divided as to whether the expression of intense emotions, especially anger and aggression, leads to a catharsis and therefore diminishes the probability of future outbreaks of anger, or whether it establishes a pattern that leads to anger being expressed more often. Clearly, these two points of view are diametrically opposed, and there have been many research studies attempting to determine which is true. The implications are enormous. If, for example, watching violence on television has a cathartic function, then it will decrease the likelihood that a viewer will go out and do something violent. On the other hand, if it reinforces the habit of aggression or violence, then watching it may lead the viewer to act out such feelings in the real world. It is healthy to express some amount of anger and frustration, but when the expression becomes habitual, then it is no longer cleansing, but self-defeating.

Couples who indulge themselves in repetitive patterns of fighting are doing themselves a grave disservice. They will eventually exhaust themselves, will never resolve anything, and will build into the marriage a chronic pattern of tension and negativity. Under the guise of communication, this is exactly what happens in so many marriages today. Individuals think they're trying to get a message across to their spouse, but the subtext is "I'm angry and you're to blame." Couples would probably be a lot better off if they just vented their anger directly and honestly without the pretense of communication.

There are a number of reasons why the expression of intense negative feelings is so difficult for people. First, as children we are often taught that it is bad to get angry. For some individuals, then, anger and the impulse to fight trigger a sense of guilt based on moral and ethical teachings stemming from childhood. For others, expressing intense emotions elicits a fear of losing control. And indeed, getting angry is a loss of control, though typically it's not nearly as dangerous as one might think. Nevertheless, there are individuals who feel most secure when they have a tight rein on their emotions. For them, letting go is frightening, because they're not sure where it's going to lead or how "crazy" they might become.

Gerard is married to a vivacious and emotionally volatile woman. Their patterns of fighting are repetitious because of his difficulty in expressing anger. Cleo, his wife, complains, "I look like the bitch, because every time I get angry, he sits there calmly taking it. That just makes me feel more guilty, and I get even madder at him. It's a vicious circle, and I don't know how to change it." It would be nice if Cleo could just stop what she's doing, but that is difficult for her. And Gerard would be better off if he were not so contained. "I've never been able to explode, have an outburst, even get mildly pissed. Maybe I enjoyed being the 'good boy' at home for so long, it's become a habit. I know Cleo would like me to, and maybe that's why I don't." The truth is that Gerard himself is so filled with anger that he is terrified by what he could do if he ever let go. In the meantime, his refusal to fight at all creates an unfortunate situation in which Cleo is made to feel as if she's a "bad" woman. If Gerard can be convinced to explore his lack of assertiveness, he will become more expressive, which will finally release Cleo from being the only emotional one of the pair.

Letting go and expressing negative feelings leaves one in a very vulnerable state, feeling defenseless and at the very least looking foolish. Another reason for keeping a lid on one's emotions is that getting angry at someone else may trigger retaliation. Many of us had the experience in childhood of getting angry and then being severely punished by our parents. Because of this, even as adults we hear an inner voice warning us, "Don't get angry or you'll be punished."

Couples who wish to take a fresh look at their attitudes about fights must examine the two ends of the continuum we have been exploring. First, are you so scared that you can't show any intense negative feelings and keep yourself bottled up inside? Or are you involved in repetitive battles that are disguised as attempts to communicate with your spouse but are really expressions of anger and hostility?

The ideal pattern falls somewhere in between. If you are too bottled up, you are operating out of a fear that will only lead to grudging truces and in some instances set you up to be the victim of a spouse who is far less inhibited in the expression of such feelings. If, on the other hand, you have been constantly angry at your mate over a period of years and your complaints are falling on deaf ears, it's time either to accept the fact that he or she is never going to change, or to seek marital counseling. The worst thing you can do is nothing, for then you only continue in an atmosphere of growing disenchantment and bitterness.

The most constructive way to relieve negative emotions is to express our personal feelings of hurt rather than reciting a litany of accusations or complaints. "You always do such-and-such" only serves to make our partner defensive, and it usually triggers an angry salvo back. Feelings of anger always cover our feelings of hurt, and the only function they perform is to release tension. The problem is that our anger makes it difficult for our partner to respond in a more sensitive and understanding way. Anger only begets anger, when what we need is compassionate understanding of how and why we are feeling hurt. Talking about hurt doesn't stimulate angry retaliation, and it gives our partner an opportunity to recognize our feelings. Being direct and honest about these feelings brings us closer, while anger only pushes us farther apart.

STYLES OF FIGHTING

The Bully

We have all known bullies at one time or another in our life. When we were children, there were always those kids who attempted to get their way by intimidating others. As we grow up, bullies either mellow or they learn to express their hostility in more socially acceptable forms. Some remain intimidating, however, often with their spouses in marriage. Additionally, there are bullies whose need to dominate and get their way only surfaces as adults and only in the context of a male-female relationship.

The psychological explanation for why some people need to push other people around is that they need to bolster their self-esteem at other people's expense. If they are "top dog" they feel better about themselves, even though everyone around them usually thinks otherwise. But there is another reason why people bully, and that is simply to discharge anger and tension.

Philip was a 46-year-old physician married to Edie, age 42 and a recent graduate of a prestigious law school. Prone to anger and hostility most of his life, Philip had developed a slightly humorous manner of expression that barely concealed the barbs he directed toward everyone, especially his wife. Edie, who was just as bright as her husband, was forever being put down by him for not being well-read and well-informed about current events, and for being too "silly" at social gatherings. For years, he seemed to take a secret delight in publicly humiliating her. At first, Edie took it. But as the years went on, and she became more intellectually self-assured, she became fed up. When she fought back and confronted him, his typical retort was: "Look, you knew what I was like when you married me. If you don't like it you can leave." They tried counseling, but all she got out of it was a lot of theory from the therapist about Philip's insecurity and his fear of her newfound success. Moreover, he could not acknowledge such fears. The pattern of hostility did not change.

When Edie sought counseling for herself, she was forced to examine a basic fear that had to be conquered before any attempts at change might be effective. Edie had to look at the "worst-case scenario" which was holding her back. In this instance, she was afraid that if she fought back, she would win the battle and lose the war, meaning Philip would leave her. Edie would never be effective unless she could emotionally accept his leaving as a possibility, no matter how slim.

This basic understanding—that there are times when one must say, "I will no longer tolerate what is going on between the two of us,"—is absolutely essential to make an impact and stimulate subsequent change. You must mean it. We're not talking about idle threats or hysterical ultimatums. When you feel deep down in your heart that you will accept the consequences of your declaration, only then will it be heard by the other person. It's not something you can fake. We know it's scary to do this. Many husbands and wives toss around words like "divorce," but actually contemplating it or risking it is another matter altogether. Nevertheless, there are tensions in relationships that will never be resolved by traditional attempts at communication, but only by action.

So, armed with a deepened sense of resolve, Edie was then instructed to do something that sounds extreme but really isn't. One of the most powerful ways we learn moral lessons is when "the shoe is on the other foot"—when we see what it's like to be on the receiving end of bullying behavior for example. Edie was told she needed to do this with Philip, that no other attempts would have an impact. The next time she was at a party, she jokingly made a comment about a political candidate while Philip was talking. It was an innocent remark, but Philip blew up and called her "stupid and juvenile." Tearfully but forcefully she then turned to him and said, "I'm fed up with you and your mean mouth. I'm just as bright as you, just as accomplished, and I'm not going to take that abuse. You're a weakling, Philip." And with that, she grabbed her purse and coat and walked out. When Philip came home later, he was furious, almost struck her, and ranted on for at least an hour about how humiliated he was and how he could never see those people again. She merely listened for a while, said, "Now you know," and went to sleep in the den. They didn't talk for weeks, until Philip gradually moved closer, uttered some oblique apologies, and clearly was a changed man with her. They are still married today.

It should come as no great surprise that most bullies in marriage are men. Because of their physical strength, it is much easier for men to be dominant. Most women are naturally frightened by the possibility of a physical confrontation because they are smaller. But there are some women who are bullies themselves—they are just more verbal and less physical in their attacks. The wife who endlessly harangues her husband is, in effect, bullying him. She knows he will eventually acquiesce to her demands.

Bea, 52, was a housewife married to Donald, a building contractor specializing in remodeling homes. They had been married for seventeen years and in all that time she had never really been satisfied with his level of success. Although they had always lived fairly well, there had been inevitable ups and downs in his business. Instead of accepting what Donald had accomplished, Bea envied what friends of theirs had. Her envy and frustration frequently erupted in the form of sarcasm and overt criticism of Donald. As he described it, "She is relentless, always reminding me of the deals that went sour, always talking about the trips everyone else is taking, the clothes, the cars, the new houses they have. I don't even fight back anymore, I just try to tune her out, but then it gets worse.

There are times when she even criticizes me in front of other people. My friends look embarrassed for me and I feel emasculated." In spite of Donald's suppressed rage, he and Bea did make up after these episodes and even had good times together. But lately his anger had been manifested in a lack of sexual desire for Bea, which was what brought the two of them into marriage counseling. Like so many individuals in marriage, Donald hoped that the process of airing his complaints in the presence of a third person would magically cause his wife to change. It didn't happen. Even when she became more aware of her long-standing insecurities it didn't break the pattern of sarcasm and biting criticism.

Donald was given advice which seemed rather extreme. First, he had to stop defending himself and make no further attempts to reason with Bea. Second, he had to take responsibility for staying in the marriage and allowing himself to be humiliated and depreciated in the way he was. Whenever she started to attack him, Donald was told to leave the room he was in, even if they were in a public place or with friends. In effect, Donald had to demonstrate that he would no longer take it. That meant he couldn't talk about resolve, he had to actually show it.

Initially Donald resisted, insisting that if he left it made him feel worse, as though he were punishing himself. Gradually, he realized that his new behavior was having more of an impact on her than he first suspected. In order to employ this strategy, Donald had to separate himself from her not only physically, but also emotionally, and that was most difficult for him. Taking this kind of action made him realize that it was his dependency upon Bea, not his love, that was the strongest tie he felt with her. He had never been conscious of this need until he forced himself to face disconnecting from her. After four or five incidents, Bea, though she was furious at first, gradually ceased her behavior.

In both of these examples, you can see that the critical catalyst for change is the "victim" who was able to tolerate fear of disconnection from the bully. We're not suggesting that people who take abuse somehow want it. What keeps bully and victim together is not pain, but the fear of being alone. In both of these cases, the extreme measures taken became milestones in the marriage and had dramatic effects. By taking responsibility and getting away from the traditional "we need to talk about this" solution, the individuals were able to have a major impact on their spouse. Taking actions that create ripple effects and then major changes in the marriage system is what works for many couples.

The Passive-Aggressive Personality

There is another kind of fighter in marriages who appears to be the opposite of the bully but is nevertheless just as infuriating and impervious to ordinary communication and conflict resolution. Paradoxically, this person fights by not fighting, by holding back and remaining impassive while his or her spouse becomes increasingly incensed over the lack of response. Quite often this person is excessively rational and overcontrolled. The origin of such behavior is often in the power struggles that existed between parent and child regarding toilet training, when the child refused to give in to parental demands. The passive-aggressive person acts out resentment or anger by being sullen, quiet, and stubborn. Sometimes a passive-aggressive person will endlessly enrage his or her mate by procrastinating or deliberately forgetting to do some little thing that the mate has patiently requested scores of time.

To be on the receiving end of such an individual's behavior is at best chronically irritating, and at worst infuriating. Often the situation reaches the point where one person begins to feel perpetually angry—like a "bitch" or "tyrant" —dealing with this innocent person, the "nice guy" whether man or woman, who means well. While this pattern can be common in marriages, when it gets out of hand, it reaches unbelievable emotional heights.

Robert was a 35-year-old business consultant. His practice had never done very well. His wife of nine years, Becky, was totally responsible for their child's care and their general financial well-being. Robert had never managed money well and invariably suffered heavy losses in the stock market. Fights over money are common to many families, as is the pattern where the wife takes over bill-paying and other financial responsibilities. What infuriated Becky was not their fights, but the style in which Robert chose to fight. "He sits there with a blank expression, makes feeble promises, and when I press him for a real plan, he never follows through. I'm starting to get crazy with all this. Either I'm furious with his silences, or I'm worried about money. Nothing I do has any impact anymore. I've tried to communicate in every way possible."

Becky was ready to throw in the towel by the time she sought counseling, which she explored because of the increasing frequency of her migraine headaches. Her physician determined that the level of anger she was experiencing was posing a serious threat to her health. In counseling, she realized that her pleading and rages were obviously not working. In order to take stronger action that might have an impact, she had to deal with emotional separation from Robert. At first, she insisted this had already occurred, but later she came to see that her anger and insistence on his "hearing" her was partly a way of staying connected. If she backed off, she would have to face being alone for the first time in their relationship, and that prospect was very frightening to her. It was suggested that she take over as much of the family finances as possible and inform Robert that she was no longer going to discuss any issues with him or have any contact until they sat down with a marriage counselor. The only way she could take control of her own destiny was to disengage emotionally. Disengagement couldn't be a game, it had to be for real; otherwise Robert would sense this was merely another empty threat. Moreover, she was told not to do this in an angry way, but coolly, calmly, and with unswerving determination.

She did all of this. Initially Robert treated it as a game, and then he started to erupt, really for the first time, with overt rather than passive anger. After three weeks, he started to come around, and then they both entered counseling for a period of six months. Finally they were able to understand each other better and to work out a plan of mutual parental and financial responsibility with Becky as the one setting the times for "meetings." Only by dramatically breaking her own response patterns could she have had this impact.

The Threatener

A surefire way to disarm one's spouse is by going straight to the edge of the marriage pact. There are husbands and wives who, when confronted by their mates, hurl a threat that will stop most people: "If you don't like it, you can leave," or "If you keep this up, we should get a divorce." The threatener is really another type of bully who uses a tactic that is as threatening as verbal or even physical abuse. Any argument will trigger World War III. Sometimes the bully means it, and other times it is just a very effective way to shut down his or her spouse. In either case, the threat is usually unwarranted and is a prime example of overkill in an argument or fight. Obviously, there are individuals whose battling has gone on for so long and seems so intractable that a divorce is seen as a real solution. But here we're talking about husbands and wives who have no serious intention of leaving and do not really wish their spouse to leave. They are merely dropping psychological bombs to get their way.

The spouse of the threatener may appear equally angry, may fight back with even louder and more intense screaming, but underneath, he or she is frightened. The threatener senses the spouse's fear, and that is why the threatener employs this tactic. He or she knows it is effective and sees the shock and terror etched on the "victim's" face.

Penny, age 29 and married for five years to Terrence, was a threatener. Throughout their marriage, they had had sexual problems. She had always been somewhat inhibited, and he had always wanted more frequent sexual contact. Whenever they had a discussion or fight about this matter, she would not listen to his feelings and invariably responded with "I can't stand this anymore—why don't you just divorce me?" Terrence typically responded, "I don't want a divorce. I love you, and I don't see why we can't work it out." After hearing that, Penny typically maintained a stony silence. Terrence was left feeling demolished, with no idea what to do next. This pattern was repeated over and over again.

Terrence clearly needed to try something different. He didn't want to play games, and he didn't want to initiate divorce proceedings. He had to take a fresh look at his relationship and understand that his wife was just who she was. In fact, he had known what her sexual attitudes were going in to the marriage. Terrence had to take responsibility for the kind of partner he chose and then confront some issues within himself. Did he want to stay with her? Could he stop badgering her for the kind of sexual contact he wanted even though he knew his demands were realistic? And finally, could he change the marriage system by backing off and becoming more his own person? He had to stretch for a level of autonomy and independence that he secretly believed was beyond his reach. If he wanted change, this was his only option. But again, it had to be for real; he couldn't pretend he was no longer interested in sex. Instead, he had to genuinely withdraw that need from the marriage for a long enough time for Penny to sense something different was really happening. And gradually, she did. After a while, she did initiate sex more than she ever had before. His backing off gave her breathing room, decreased tensions, and helped her see the positive connection between feeling relaxed and sexual desire. He was instructed to respond to her sexual overtures but without suddenly changing his expectations. In time, she sensed all these changes in him, and became worried about his loyalty to the marriage. This worry of hers reduced her use of threats and motivated her to work on relaxation. Eventually they were able to work out a compromise that was comfortable for them both.

The Psychological Battler

A new kind of fighter has emerged on the marriage scene in the last few decades—the psychological battler. This is a person who, in the guise of rational communication, tries to obscure issues with the relentless use of logic, psychological analysis, and skilled character assassination. Armed with the latest in "psychobabble," this type of fighter can make his or her spouse absolutely furious and at a loss for words. The point, of course, is precisely that—to counter any real communication or discussion with attacks on the other person's character.

Derek and Cynthia had been married for seventeen years. He was a junior college history instructor, and she was a supervising nurse at a hospital. Whenever they had a fight about anything, Derek very quickly assaulted his wife with clearly delineated reasons why she obviously hated men and had no conception of love, intimacy, or honest communication. In the early years, she tried to fight back, even becoming a bit of a screamer, all to no avail. He was just too clever, too verbally facile.

Cynthia was too dependent upon the relationship to let go of the fight. Whenever she did, she felt alone, threatened by his dark picture of her, and then got back into the fight again. She kept playing into the fighting for the most common of reasons—the desire to prove that she was right and he was wrong about her. However, when it was suggested to her that she just stop talking to him about emotionally laden issues, things began to change. She let Derek know that unless he was willing to argue about the issues alone without attacking her personality and belittling her views, she would have to remain aloof, and she did. Because she could now be independent, Derek began to see how dependent he was on her. In the past, his dependency had been hidden behind his rhetoric; as long as he could keep her self-esteem low, he knew she would never leave him. Cynthia radically altered the balance of forces in the marriage by beginning to highlight his dependency rather than hers. Only then did Derek slowly modify his way of communicating.

AVOIDING FIGHTS

We fight not only as a way of handling conflict but also as a way of staying connected and getting our mate to validate our position. Too often, we not only need to win, we need our mate to acknowledge that win. To the degree we are Other-Directed, we allow ourselves to fall prey to the fantasy of being able to directly change our mate and how our mate responds to us.

Intense and persistent fights are commonplace in marriages, but they demand uncommon solutions. All of the examples we've described suggest that massive and radical attempts to upset the marriage system are often what is needed. More traditional techniques may be effective in marriages that feature milder and less volatile types of arguments, as discussed in Chapter 3, on change. But when fighting gets out of hand, the goal must be breaking patterns rather than conflict resolution. The latter implies that issues will be discussed and worked out in a rational fashion. But most of us are not that reasonable, especially when we are at odds with our mate.

There are ways to short-circuit the tension-argument-fight sequence. We do not have to respond automatically or take the bait as we so often do. For example, fights are often triggered by one person's responding to another's mood, when the first person could just as well ignore the other's mood, or with kindness and compassion ask if anything is wrong. The husband who comes home only to be greeted by a wife who seems agitated or depressed about something may suddenly become a scapegoat if he criticizes her mood. How much more effective it would be if he just acknowledged her mood and went into another room. Sometimes, humor can be disarming or tension-relieving. Both husbands and wives, when they are in a foul mood, are prone to "dump" on their mates. That common tendency need not be the beginning of a battle. Short-circuiting fights requires that we not take personally every negative mood or emotion expressed by our spouse. More often than not, it has nothing to do with us or anything we've done.

For some couples, fighting may not be an intolerable activity. They may even enjoy it, partly as a way of releasing tensions. But for many people fighting may be destructive and demoralizing. When this is the case, what is needed to change the fighting pattern is autonomy and emotional disengagement. It is essential to learn to tolerate disconnection. In order to detach emotionally in this fashion, one must have the courage to experience aloneness.

Tolerating disconnection also enables individuals to let go of the need to initiate fights. The urge to attack, belittle, or criticize is overwhelming at times. It also makes people feel out of control, which is frightening. But there is a sense of satisfaction that emerges when one conquers the impulse to ram the "truth" down someone's throat. Acceptance rather than criticism or attack is ultimately much more gratifying.

We certainly do not advocate trial separations as the best solution to intense marital conflicts. But the fact that brief temporary separations are often effective does provide some clues to why men and women engage in intense and heated fighting on a daily basis. The fear of being alone, of feeling isolated or abandoned, is at the core of intense fights. Wives and husbands are not just trying to win the fight, they are unconsciously trying to stay connected to each other. This primitive wish is more powerful than rational attempts to end the conflict. That is why when there is a mandatory disengagement, couples will often see the relationship more clearly, including what is positive about it, and remember why they fell in love in the first place.

When clashing gets so out of hand that disengagement is impossible when living under the same roof, it can be worthwhile to consider a trial separation for a few weeks, even a few months. It can work. Separation often provides the most dramatic contrast between the fleeting and illusory rewards of fighting and the poignant and potentially irreversible losses that such conflicts can create. However, staying apart for more than three months can put the marriage in jeopardy. We are not suggesting that one of you must move out of the house, but that you try to separate emotionally for a time in order to become Self-Directed. Only then will the storm clouds clear up and will each person gain a new perspective on the marriage.

Every marriage ultimately requires a sense of our own value, a feeling of self-determination, and an awareness of our basic entitlements. We all really know what is good for us and what robs us of dignity and self-respect. Trusting this knowledge and making it operative, while never easy for any of us, will work. It will change the fight pattern, and it will ultimately be effective.

We often hear couples justifying their fighting on the grounds that they do it out of love! What they mean is that the caring they have toward their spouse is so powerful that they cannot conceive of standing back and disconnecting emotionally, taking a fresh look or finding a new tack. The opposite is really more accurate. When you truly love your mate, you won't hold up a mirror for your mate to see the painful effects of his or her outbursts or losses of control. Lovers fight, but genuine and mature love often tells us when and how not to fight. Loving a husband or wife often means you do what is not only best for you, but what is most growth-enhancing for you as a couple.

CHAPTER SIX

Work and Money: Solving New Dilemmas

The decade of the 1980s began with American society savoring the financial rewards of work. We were obsessed with work in order to spend and to have all those things that signified success. The decade is ending with the emergence of a new ethic—prudence, conservatism, and an underlying fear of not being able to keep up with the standards of living we have set for ourselves.

Work and money dominate the lives of all adults in general and married people in particular. But the preoccupations with accomplishment, achievement, and acquisition have failed to enrich the lives of husbands and wives or to bring our families closer together. Our careers may have allowed us to buy more material goods but they haven't brought us much in the way of happiness or peace of mind.

We have come to believe that "we are what we do," and we've directed most of our energies into work. And, today, while the financial payoff still exists, the emotional rewards of work seem to be diminishing, yet we still carry on, and not just because we need to.

A recent survey of male and female business executives posed the question "What would you do if you inherited enough money to retire comfortably?" The vast majority said they would continue working at their current jobs. But fewer than 10 percent of those executives said this choice to continue working was related to the fact that they actually enjoyed their work! What then keeps their noses tied to the grindstone?

The Greek word for work, *ponos*, has a dual meaning—it also is the word for sorrow. Essentially, the Greeks saw work as an unfortunate curse and enemy of one's free spirit. Early Hebrews and Christians viewed work as a punishment for sin, although the Christians broadened the definition somewhat to include the notion of charity. Thus work also became a means of lending assistance to someone in need.

It wasn't until Saint Thomas Aquinas that work was imbued with any notion of real worth. He carefully devised a hierarchy of trades and professions based upon what he saw as their value to the community. The Protestant Reformation once again redefined work as a way of better serving God. Work was not simply an inevitable drudgery or a penalty for sins, it was seen as worthy and divine service.

More recently, Western culture has moved away from the concept of work as service to a divine being and moved toward an understanding of work as a means to achieve self-realization and fulfillment. When we work, we define ourselves and sharpen our identity through our products and achievements.

THE MEANING OF WORK

The current emphasis on work in our culture has little to do with its roots in physical survival. Many of us have become workaholics, using our accomplishments in work as the primary tool to shape our self-image. From work we hope to find answers to a variety of questions:

> Am I respected?
> Am I effective?
> Am I intelligent?
> Am I talented?
> Am I worthy?
> Am I loved?

Work has the effect of changing or reshaping things. Work gives us a vivid and concrete idea of who we are, because it provides us with a context in which to test and measure ourselves.

Most basically, in our work we gain a sense of personal value from feeling capable. Competence, effectiveness, and power are almost synonymous terms in our culture. As small children we felt valued because of the adoring love and attention of our parents. But as we get older, feeling valued requires more than simply being cute and our parent's children. Self-esteem, if it is to continue to grow, depends increasingly upon what we do to be respected. And when we are competent in our work we bask in its by-products—admiration and respect.

In our love relationships at home, our wish for validation and affection may far outstrip what we actually receive from our mates. One solution to this painful emotional dilemma is to compensate for those basic needs for love and security through our work. For many, the energy and devotion so willingly given to work is, in reality, a disguised attempt to create a sense of love, affection, even family.

HUSBANDS AND WORK

Regardless of one's profession or occupation today, it is necessary to work much harder just to stay even. The middle class in America is being squeezed by diverse economic forces. A major influence is the upward shift in life-style expectations that has been occurring gradually. In the past, we counted on inflation to carry us along, increasing the value of our homes, for example, and therefore making us feel richer and more secure. Prior to 1980, people naively felt their jobs would remain stable and their professions healthy, and they believed their confidence about the future was appropriate. Those days are over. We have entered a period in which every profession is either overcrowded, constricted by new regulations, or in a state of flux and chaos because of the changes going on in corporate America. Rising expectations and easy upward mobility are things of the past. And we're all having difficulty adjusting to this.

Husbands today are working harder simply to maintain the status quo. And with the attendant increased mental pressure, they are finding themselves much less likely to take home for granted. Men are more likely to view their marriage and home life as a sanctuary from the outside world. One man said, "I don't have the perfect marriage, but I guess nobody does. I try to overlook the flaws and concentrate on the things that are good."

Unforthcoming as men are about feelings, it is in the area of financial responsibility that they have been most outspoken. Because women have so vehemently, and somewhat successfully, fought for equal opportunity and pay, men now expect women to share that burden with them. It shouldn't surprise anyone that finances are the one issue men will talk about. Remember, a man's focus on work doesn't come out of a vacuum. He has been taught that his very value lies in his success or failure in that domain. He has also learned through countless experiences that his attractiveness to women is largely a product not of sweetness and sensitivity but of effectiveness and strength. Most men are not driven so much by a wish for success as by a haunting fear of failure. No wonder they devote so much attention to work-related issues.

For men, being able to say they're "somebody" has been an eternal driving quest central to their feelings of masculinity. The heart of how they define themselves is their work, irrespective of what they do in addition to their jobs.

Men live in a world in which they are expected to be aggressive. It's not that women cannot also be aggressive, for they certainly can be and are, but being aggressive is more an imperative for men and an option for women. Men learn from early childhood the connections between autonomy, aggressiveness, competence, and a sense of masculinity. And for a man, there is little else that rivals the crucial importance of a masculine identity.

Men are different from women in a fundamental way. Unlike girls, boys are required to separate themselves from the warmth and safety of their mothers in order to begin the long and gradual process of identity formation. Girls can stay closely attached to the mother while they model their behavior after hers; boys must break away from her and look to the father as a role model. Boys learn about aggression and competition from their fathers, while girls learn about cooperation and relationships from their mothers. The lingering effects of these early experiences can still be clearly seen in adulthood in the ways men and women relate to the balance between work and love. Men have been taught that strength and power come from being assertive, actively "doing." Women, on the other hand, because they are more closely bound to their mothers, associate "being" and relatedness with strength. Women tend to have more close friends throughout their lives than do men. For women, friendships are a wonderful bank of strength, support, and nurturance from which they can easily draw. Men tend to have acquaintances instead, and the thought of looking to a man friend for support is sadly something that makes many men feel uncomfortable. That is why men often continue to bolster their self-esteem and salve emotional wounds by throwing themselves into work.

One possible by-product of the sexual and feminist revolutions was the erosion of "masculine" territories. If sexual conquest was no longer a way for men to define themselves, then why not throw themselves into work and its accomplishments? It is no accident that men in their thirties, those most influenced by the women's movement, are the ones who have been most obsessed by work and achievement. In what other area can a man still feel "manly"?

We all feel enormous pressures and anxiety in work. But men and women handle these concerns in different ways. When a woman feels overwhelmed with pressures and worries, she looks for solace, feedback, and support from the network of friends she is careful to maintain or from her husband if she perceives him as reassuring. Men react differently, and find themselves withdrawing from the relationship when they are under extreme work pressures. Women often take this behavior personally or mistakenly conclude that their husbands are incapable of intimacy.

When men retreat during times of pressure they are not attempting to shut their mates out, they are trying to retain their strength and resolve. It is unfortunate, but men have systematically been taught that strength comes from containing feelings rather than acknowledging or talking about them.

Lee, a man in his late forties, shook his head and said, "I go through periods at work when I feel totally overwhelmed, and I know it's those times when I pull away from Janet. It's strange. I know she's there and would do anything to help me—she even understands a lot because she's going through similar problems herself at work—but I can't seem to open up to her. She thinks I don't trust her or value what she says or that I'm just plain afraid of being close, but honestly I'm afraid that if I started I wouldn't stop. I'd turn into this weakling. So I shut up, keep it to myself, and just try and handle it."

Lee's difficulty is not so much that he is uncomfortable with closeness, but that he is afraid that the release of pent-up feelings will have the net effect of weakening rather than strengthening him. And for men, this uneasiness is not all that irrational. In male stress management studies, competence-building strategies appear to be much more effective in warding off stress than do simplistic suggestions that merely emphasize simple relaxation and "opening up." Men don't consciously choose to be strong; they feel an unconscious need to be strong. But Lee's task is to discover the value of more emotional balance in his life. If he learns to trust Janet, he will find that closeness can actually be replenishing and strengthening. Developing a sense of trust requires small steps. When Lee begins to reveal more of his inner thoughts and concerns, rather than feeling weakened or humiliated, he will feel supported and understood by Janet.

Even more important than a man's need to feel strong is his need to feel like a winner. It is not enough to have tried; men feel they must also succeed. Whereas most women feel they have a choice about having a career, men are painfully aware that they have no real latitude; they must be self-sufficient. And they often feel they will be judged by the *level* of success they achieve.

In our culture, the most important concrete indicator of success is money. Unfortunately, this singular focus on money, work, and success leaves men with limited resources for self-esteem and value. As women work more, the special importance of men's contribution has diminished and become less mysterious and important. It is true that men are participating more in all areas of family life and are slowly finding new ways of feeling valued. But we are in a time of tremendous flux, and none of men's other activities, regardless of how successful they may be at them, have yet assumed the tremendous importance of work.

It is for this reason that midlife poses so many problems for men. It's not so much that they feel they have missed something, and it's not simply that they are burned out. It's that they don't feel they are moving ahead in their work situation with respect to their peers. In their twenties, men still feel like kids, as if their whole life is ahead of them. The thirties are a time of vitality, plans, and dreams; often a time of rapid career advancement accompanied by a real feeling of success or at least having a shot at it. But during the midforties, something very different happens: resignation sets in. There is much less room at the top than there was in the middle, and progress slows. The awareness of a career plateau and the closing of doors becomes a painful, if silent, reality. Because so much of a man's identity is tied up with work, he feels inadequate when his career stagnates.

It is at this time that men need to develop new ways of feeling good about themselves that are totally independent of their job situations. They need to be aware that they are moving through a difficult experience but one that is also shared by other men. For if they don't, they will be vulnerable to acting out the often impulsive and self-defeating patterns so frequently associated with "midlife crisis." Husbands who are able to share inner feelings and concerns with their wives rarely venture outside the marriage seeking illusory solutions to their problems. Interestingly enough, as couples feel more committed to their marriages, we hear less talk of midlife crisis. Men are moving in the direction of intimacy and mutual support. They are also beginning to find new sources of gratification, the best example of which is today's renewed emphasis on children and family life.

WOMEN AND WORK

In nearly 50 percent of all marriages, the wife works. Having given up the traditional roles of full-time mothering and homemaking, these women have taken on the additional challenge of working. But, what has it cost them? What are the mixed feelings? What are the rewards?

There is probably nothing else so demanding and exhausting and yet so virtually impossible to measure as mothering. But that was the role and the destiny girls were traditionally taught to fulfill. One woman eloquently stated, "We were trained to look out for everybody else's needs first, and then if there was anything left over we could take care of ourselves." As we've discussed, mothers are typically the prime movers for making it all possible.

It was no accident that mothering became a feminist issue. Mothering involves love, encouragement, selflessness, and empathy, but it is not an activity that leads to an expanding definition of self, nor is it any sure path to power or the realization of potential.

There is no doubt that women have proved themselves every bit as capable as men in the workplace. But sometimes we must be careful about what we wish for, because it might just come true, as it did for women! Certainly women gained access to power, respect, and admiration through work, but not without cost. Work rapidly became not an option but an expectation, and what once felt like an exhilarating challenge to women has become a juggling act fraught with more pressures than men experience.

As long as a dual-career-oriented couple focus upon their respective work situations, there are relatively few problems. They may have more frequent separations because of conflicting schedules and commitments, but these complexities can even have the effect of keeping the marriage fresh and stimulating. Such marriages may suffer from a lack of time together, but the compensation is that they are enhanced by the understanding that comes from having to struggle with similar experiences. Even couples who wish to retain some independence—perhaps the wife retains her maiden name, or the couple maintain separate bank accounts—still feel a sense of closeness and common purpose.

Problems may arise, however, when a woman's sense of independence is compromised by the inevitable sacrifices that accompany the realities of beginning a family. Having a child is rarely disruptive to a man's career. Their wives simply have the children, they become fathers, and life goes on without so much as a ripple. For the woman, it is quite different. She is forced to ask herself some very confusing and painful questions: Do I get pregnant, keep working, have my baby, and then go back to work after a couple of months off? Do I decrease our income by stopping work? How will I feel if I give up my career? Will I be able to resume it later? How will my husband feel if I want to stop working? How important is it for me to spend time with my children when they are young? And on and on. Obviously, these are questions that are logically posed to both the man and the woman. But women often feel that even if the issues are discussed, it is her central responsibility to think them through, for they affect her life in strikingly different ways than they do the man's.

Randi, at 24 recently married, works in the television industry. She and her husband would like to start a family, but she has serious concerns about her commitment to children and the time she would be willing to devote to them. She says, "My mother was wonderful—always there when I came home from school and always encouraging and happy to spend her time helping me when I needed it. I know, without the slightest doubt, I couldn't have done what

I've done if she hadn't provided the foundation. I'm very ambitious, and I like what I do. I hate to admit it, but I don't think I'd be willing to give all this up and spend anywhere near the time with my child that my mother did with me, and I worry about what kind of effect that's going to have."

Randi is right to worry. Her husband is going to have to take up a lot of slack, and he is as ambivalent about doing it as she is. Caring for children properly does take an enormous amount of time and attention to detail. Children flourish with deeply interested, available parents, and conversely they develop a variety of problems in homes where parents are self-involved, distracted, or absent. The hard, unadorned truth is that it is extremely difficult to "have it all," for it is hard to be committed to a demanding career and also be a wife and a mother who participates fully in her child's day-to-day activities unless the father is equally generous with his time and involvement.

The sheer exhaustion caused by what women must juggle creates tension and conflict. Victoria, who is 40 and has two children, met her husband while they were both in medical school. They had always dreamed of opening a pediatric practice in a small town and finally have reached that goal. "Now," Victoria explains, "while my children are still young, I'd like to spend more time with them when they really need me. When I talk about this with Bob, he throws a fit, says, 'But you're a doctor,' and accuses me of breaking our deal. I guess the real truth is that at this time in my life I'm a lot more interested in my children's welfare than I am in medicine. What I'd really like to do is quit the practice and stay home and be a mom."

Victoria, like so many women, is physically and emotionally drained by trying to excel at everything. Unfortunately, something has to give. For her, giving up or scaling down her career makes sense, but it also creates resentment on the part of her husband, who took her at her word when she agreed to be his partner in full-time practice. And resentment in her situation is not one-sided. In turn, Victoria is angry that Bob doesn't make more of an attempt to try to see things her way and isn't more understanding and receptive about her wanting to spend additional time at home with their children. Victoria and Bob need to understand that change is a part of marriage and that rigid expectations only result in interminable clashes. Victoria must accept the legitimacy of Bob's disappointment and underlying financial concerns and at the same time attempt to scale down her hours. Bob has to become more sympathetic to the difficult reality of a woman's struggle between career and family.

Women have always selected mates on the basis of success and power—the more successful and accomplished, the more valued. This age-old selection process has changed little, despite the fact that women have entered the work force and created their own achievements. But there is a new problem. Women assumed when they began to work that men would value their energy and success in a similar fashion—a logical but woefully inaccurate assumption. Because men were never taught to define themselves in terms of a woman's prestige or success, they do not put any particular value on it.

This striking disappointment has caused women a great deal of consternation and resentment. As one woman poignantly observed, "I've worked my tail off, worked just as hard as my husband has, and I haven't gotten a whole lot of credit for it. I feel proud of what I've been able to do, and he seems to take it totally for granted. The most I get is a 'now you know how tough it is out there' from him. It makes me sad, because I expected more."

It is clear that for many women the sweet promise of fulfillment as a natural outgrowth of work has faded. It's not that work doesn't have important payoffs, but it's burdensome and exhausting as well. In many ways, women have it much tougher than men. The conditioning men received at least was clear and consistent, and by and large, men never expected to work and also be intensely involved in being a parent. Women must make more painful decisions regarding the distribution of their time and energy. Do they drive themselves ahead in their careers, mimicking their workaholic male counterparts, and forgo mothering altogether? Do they have a child, rest awhile, and hope to resume their careers without having lost too much speed and momentum? Do they bend their needs for autonomy and participate more fully in the mothering experience? Obviously none of these questions is easy to answer, but it is not intelligence or capability that separates the experiences of men and women; it is women's unique legacy, motherhood.

An increasingly common approach to these dilemmas is the notion of sequencing goals or objectives rather than attempting to juggle them simultaneously. Some women choose to leave careers or at the very least slow down dramatically, and scale down their life-styles, in order to have children and spend quality time with them. Other women put off having a family in order to make inroads in their career, consolidate achievements or bases of power, and then shift gears and focus on family life. Neither of these strategies is perfect, because each entails the giving up of certain dreams. This dilemma is especially critical for women, although it certainly affects men as well. One thing is very clear today: doing everything with a full emotional and intellectual commitment is impossible.

In order for women to make this adjustment in their life-style, they must reassess their situation, sort out their priorities, and forget about trying to have it all. Millions of married women are beginning to do this, with varying degrees of success.

WORKAHOLISM

The enhancement of self primarily through work that has become a national preoccupation has had a devastating effect on many American marriages. The inherent selfishness and insularity of the workaholic shuts out intimacy and damages partnerships.

Evan had been overweight ever since he could remember. In school, even though he was quite bright, he was only an average student, because most of his energies were directed toward trying desperately to be "one of the guys" and fantasizing about the cheerleaders, who were only too glad to be his friends but nothing more. While eating was the most available gratification in his younger years, upon graduation from college he found a new one—work.

In his early thirties, Evan, a slave to grueling and driven work habits, married. Evan never felt secure in Angie's love—she was the "pretty girl" he had always dreamed about but never believed he could find or manage to hold on to. His doubt of her love made him work even harder, convinced that his success was the only thing keeping her connected to him. In fact, as he moved rapidly up the corporate ladder Angie did enjoy his growing power as well as the economic rewards that followed. The turning point came when they had their first child, an "accident" she wanted and he didn't feel ready for. Angie needed more of his time and an increased involvement at home, and he couldn't give it to her.

When Evan entered therapy, he was in a painful quandary. "I'm afraid to slack off at work for fear of losing my edge," Evan exclaimed. "But I know if I don't I'm going to lose Angie. I guess I was always afraid I'd lose her if I couldn't be the superprovider, but now it seems to be happening anyway."

Evan felt lovable only as a function of his career success, and the thought of in any way putting that in jeopardy struck terror in his heart. In his mind, Angie didn't love him, she needed him for what he could provide. When Evan painstakingly examined the powerful connection in his mind between self-worth and accomplishment, he came to realize he had never felt valued for anything other than work achievement. Work had become a safe haven. Anything that posed the slightest threat to work was seen as incredibly dangerous.

In therapy, Evan was encouraged to do two things. First, he was asked to create an open dialogue with Angie in which they explored not only what she loved and valued about him but also his fear of losing her. Second, Evan was asked to risk taking some important chances: going on the vacation he had never taken, not working weekends, and taking work home only two nights a week. At first, he was swept with waves of panic when he forced himself not to work, but gradually the anxiety subsided and was replaced with a growing and reassuring awareness that time off from work actually enriched rather than threatened his life.

The workaholic's emphasis is on control. We all have normal needs for control in our lives, but for some this need becomes exaggerated and dominant. People who love their work with a greater passion and involvement than they can love another person are typically individuals who find it difficult to love anything they cannot also control. Unlike work, love implies a willingness to relinquish control, which the workaholic systematically avoids.

"I think George would like nothing better than for me to make him the center of my life," Lydia complained, "but I refuse to do that. I've worked too hard to get where I am, and I'm not going to let anyone take away my success." Lydia felt that George had mounted an increasing campaign to sabotage her career because he was threatened by her achievements. Nothing could have been further from the truth.

"I love the fact that Lydia is successful, and I'm proud of all of her accomplishments," George responded. "It's just that I think there is a time and a place for work, and I don't think she knows how to set it aside, relax, and just be herself. I think she feels that if she isn't tough all the time, somehow she will lose all her strength and resolve. I wish that sometimes she would just let go and lighten up. I know I'd feel a whole lot closer to her."

Lydia couldn't let down, she couldn't relax. It was as if demons were in hot pursuit and if she slowed for a moment they would overtake her. Lydia grew up in a family with a passive, victimized mother imprisoned by her emotional and economic dependence upon a selfish and abusive man. Vowing at an early age to be different, Lydia had come to equate fierce independence, achievement, and toughness with safety. Tenderness and vulnerability she saw as dangerous weaknesses to be avoided at all cost.

When Lydia and George began therapy, the relationship was at the point of collapse. Lydia didn't want to give up her marriage, but was terrified of acknowledging its importance to her. Slowly, Lydia began admitting to herself, first alone and then in George's presence, the value of the relationship. At first she cringed at such admissions of need for fear George would see her as the weak person she felt herself to be inside. Instead George simply felt relief at finally making contact with the vulnerable, human side of Lydia he always had known was there but couldn't ever seem to connect with. What was critical for Lydia was to examine how she had used her focus on work essentially to avoid her fear of intimacy.

Underlying the workaholic's grasping need for control are early experiences that led to painful insecurity, feelings of inadequacy, and strong dependency fears. Work becomes the ideal solution. It is used to shore up the sense of self-worth that is not found within relationships. Closeness and the expression of tender, vulnerable feelings are terrifying for the workaholic, for they require the courage to relinquish control. Loving and sharing oneself with a mate is avoided, for it is seen as essentially depleting. Workaholics choose to invest in work rather than love because the payoff feels safer and more predictable. They hide in the work they can control and manipulate, believing that success is something they can make happen with enough diligence, time, and effort, which it often is. Love is frightening, for they know the fragile limits of their control and live in dread of being rejected by those they secretly need and care for.

Scaling up from the individual work addict, we've become a society devoted to work. Perhaps out of a fear of wanting too much from love and fearing its all too frequent failure, we have redirected our energies into the safety of work. This glorification of work sucks up not only our aggressive energies but our sexual energies as well, leaving many couples needing and wanting less from each other in this area. Couples are too tired, too frazzled, and too preoccupied to be close to each other. They come home to refuel and rest in preparation for tomorrow's demands, but what is forgotten is any real man/woman experience today.

Our expectation has been that work would somehow bring us more pleasure, that it would enhance our lives and that of our families. The fact is that work really hasn't lived up to that implicit promise. Focusing all our time and energy on work has allowed us to acquire more possessions but at the expense of the quality of life with our mates and children. "They will wait, work can't," we say, fooling only ourselves that the situation is only temporary and the means to an end. The problem is that for many of us, the means inevitably becomes the end. Our marriages drift into self-absorbed and separate experiences in which we slowly lose any meaningful contact with each other. And our children grow so quickly that we are left to quietly mourn the trips we didn't take, the talks we meant to have, and the caring and involved parental guidance we intended to provide.

The reality is that we can't do it all; we can't be a superstar at work, a terrific mate, and an involved parent. No one can. Life demands choices, which in turn imply certain resignations. We must decide what is most important and meaningful and set priorities. If we want to have a close marriage and be the kind of parents that children need, we must also be willing to give generously of ourselves.

Work is certainly easier to measure, is more simply controlled, and produces real accolades for our efforts and achievements. But what do we have in the end? It would seem a far richer solution to pull back from our fixation on work and to reinvest our energies where they really count—at home with the people we love. The payoff is surely more rewarding than the last-hurrah retirement bash and gold watch.

MONEY AND SELF-RESPECT

Money has a way of bringing out the absolute worst in people. It doesn't seem to matter whether we have a lot of money or only a little. When there is too little of it there are problems, and when there is a lot of it there are still problems.

Money means power in our culture. The person who controls the money is in a position of authority, and the person who doesn't is on the outside looking in with nose pressed to the glass. Traditionally, men firmly held the reins of power in the relationship by controlling the family finances. Many women knew little and cared less about money, and were kept in the dark by men, whose decisions were never challenged because they alone knew what was going on. Even if a man casually asked, "What do you think about refinancing the second mortgage on the house and putting the money in a bond fund, since interest rates are going down?" his wife's response was typically to throw up her hands and trust his judgment.

All that has changed. Many women know as much about finance as men do, and in many households decisions are made on a mutually informed basis. But despite the raised level of awareness and understanding of finance, problems persist. It is not information that is the difficulty, but control and trust.

Sometimes a man will insist that he hold on to the family checkbook simply because he believes control over the bank account is a male prerogative, even if he is less competent financially than his wife and routinely fails to balance the checking account. It is understandably exasperating for women who are better at handling the family money to have to tap-dance around to protect the man's ego. Why can't we all relax a bit, let go of tired old stereotypes, and just let the one who does it best do it?

One of the most common causes of frustration and tension in a marriage is the way we play out the roles of spender and saver. The fact is that most of us are not particularly good at managing money, or at saving rather than spending. Typically, one partner assumes the natural role of the spender while the other partner dons the mantle of saver. These roles are often complementary at the beginning of the marriage but can gradually become a source of conflict. Each person is utterly convinced he is right and that the other person should change his habits. The spender spends; otherwise nothing would be purchased or done. And the saver saves, convinced that if he did not take every measure to conserve, it would be tantamount to saying, "Take me to the poorhouse, and step on it!"

Whenever arguments over finances bring couples into counseling, they are typically looking for a judge who will pronounce one person guilty—either anxious and tight-fisted, or impulsive and irresponsible. The husband and wife may see themselves quite differently: the "miser" may think he or she is merely fiscally prudent, and the "spendthrift" may view himself or herself as generous and carefree. As psychologists, our task is first to clear the air of anger, tension, and accusations. When both parties see that they are just who they are rather than right or wrong, then and only then can the stage be set for sincere and effective dialogue, negotiation, and compromise. The key word here is *dialogue*, for in good marriages there is always an ongoing dialogue about money: making it, saving it, and spending it.

Many good marriages have monthly battles over finances, but ones that are characterized by basic goodwill and an acceptance of the fact that neither person is going to change all that much. Sometimes the best we can hope for is a spirited debate about family finances, with each partner compromising out of love rather than resentment.

In working with couples today, we find that fights about money are much more complicated than they were a few decades ago. Equality between men and women has forever changed the simple arrangement of man as provider and woman as the protected and secure one. Not only are marriages today composed of dual providers, but men and women are entering marriage later in life and with more of their own hard-earned assets. As a result, prenuptial arrangements are increasingly common, and for good reason. Should the woman executive who has her own home put it into joint ownership if the man she marries earns less income and has fewer assets? What about the husband who has built a profession or business for years, and now marries or remarries—should he generously give his new bride half ownership? As soon as one person answers no to these situations, a financial pact must be worked out in addition to the traditional marriage contract. This is a new fact of life that is being accepted in principle by millions of men and women. Problems arise when all the nuances of these new agreements are discussed and crop up with annoying frequency. The underlying cause for such disputes, of course, is the fear that the marriage might not last, and therefore these agreements have serious emotional implications.

These new complications are at the very least not very romantic and quite often are the source of major strains in the relationship. So what's the answer? Blind faith? No. Endless fighting and negotiation? That doesn't seem to work very well either. In our view, these thorny new considerations are becoming gradually accepted and therefore are less upsetting. Yes, there is an accompanying loss of innocence and idealism. Today, we are having to separate the concept of love from the concept of money. Less and less are we hearing, "If he really loved me, he wouldn't have me sign a prenuptial agreement." We are learning that each person has a right to his or her own money and a right to feel financially secure even as the couple enter a new marriage. It's a fact of life, and the sooner we come to accept it, the less likely couples will be to engage in fruitless battles. Indeed, in our work, we have found that those couples who are able to discuss financial matters in a calm and relatively dispassionate fashion, free of overtones about love and caring, are the very ones who also build a more solid marriage.

There is no question that couples today are having to make more complex accommodations to each other's careers and financial concerns. For both wives and husbands, work is often a real necessity as well as a source of gratification and self-esteem. We are learning to respect not only each other's work-related obligations but also our needs to pursue aspects of work for stimulation, challenge, and fulfillment. We are slowly learning to value work not simply by how much income it generates but more broadly by its importance and meaning to the person engaged in it.

And perhaps most critical, wives and husbands are recognizing that the complexities of work and money can be dealt with in a way that is not destructive and not a measure of how much they love each other.

CHAPTER SEVEN

Reawakening Sexual Desire

*T*he most closely kept secret of any marriage is what goes on in the bedroom. In marriage counseling, psychologists are immediately skeptical when they inquire of a couple about their sexual relationship and hear, "Oh, it's just fine." Why do we never believe that? The first reason is that most people lie in order to disguise the embarrassment and secret sense of inadequacy they feel. Most husbands and wives are not as satisfied in this area as they would like to be. But, for most, that dissatisfaction is not enough to seek counseling, to consider affairs, or to spend nights tossing and turning with frustration. We all tend to believe that's just the way it goes in marriage. Couples nervously laugh off their doubt and discomfort, choosing to accept that a decline in sexual interest and activity is the norm in marriage. And, in varying degrees, that's true. But contemporary marriages seem to suffer from this malaise more than ever before, which is rather odd, since we are more knowledgeable about sex than ever before and couples today are also more consciously committed.

WHAT HAPPENED TO SEX?

By the mid-1980s, it was generally acknowledged that the sexual revolution was over. In the 1960s and 1970s, the idea that sex could be not only an expression of love and caring but recreational as well was an interesting new facet of the psychology of growth and self-actualization. Because we were traditionally so sexually conservative compared with Europeans, experimentation and discovery were liberating. Men and women threw themselves into exciting, new, and heretofore forbidden experiences. By the beginning of the 1980s, however, the thrill began to wane. It was as though we had become satiated with sexual themes, activities, and talk. In retrospect, the reason for this is quite obvious. Any repeated and prolonged exposure to pleasurable stimuli invariably leads to satiation; there are only so many desserts one can eat. With sex, devoid of deeper love and commitment, this satiation effect gradually took over. Single men and women felt empty after sexual encounters—indeed, for many there was a kind of depression that followed a "one-night stand."

And married couples found that "opening up" a marriage created more insecurities and tensions than the relationship could accommodate.

The one truth that was omitted from the sexual-revolution guidebook was that sex without love is a momentarily pleasing but inevitably meaningless act. Engaging in casual sex is a poignant reminder that we don't love that person and may not even want to see him or her again. In our society, love and intimacy have always been a part of sexuality, and that realization finally sobered us and made us turn away from casual sex. So the revolution ended. But what replaced it? Did we suddenly enter a new era of renewed desire and attraction for those we did love? Unfortunately, no. We got left out in sexual limbo, and we're still there. We're more committed than ever to our spouses, but the sexual part of that union is still a bit anemic. Clinicians and counselors everywhere are talking about the dramatic increase in what is called "inhibited sexual desire" among men as well as women today. Moreover, this waning of sexual interest is not necessarily a function of aging or related to the length of the marriage. Some of those at high risk for this peculiar malaise seem to be well-educated and accomplished young people in their late twenties and thirties. On the outside, they look alive and hungry for life's adventures, but inside there is frequently a very weak drive toward sexual expression.

DISENCHANTMENT

The age-old problem in marriage is, how do you keep passion and desire alive? The cynical old saying "Marriage is the antidote to romance" suggests that as romantic feelings wane, so does sexual desire. Because romance is based on novelty and newness, and further because in the romantic phase of a relationship we are not yet certain of our lover's commitment to us, there is an ongoing yearning and desire, heightened by a tinge of anxiety. In reality, romantic sex often pales in comparison with the more secure, relaxed sexual encounters husbands and wives may have. But in romance there is always the heat generated by the tension of not knowing whether your lover will always care for and always desire you.

Even when couples are engaged or living together, there are little moments, secretly noted by both partners, that are the potential precursors to disinterest. We all remember the first time we didn't want to have sex with our lover. Regardless of whether we were bored or tired at the time, we remember it as a kind of landmark moment. One of the mainstays of romantic feeling is that whenever one partner wants to make love, the other seems to want it at the same time or, at the very least, delightfully responds to any overtures. But when the first refusal inevitably takes place, in the mind of the decliner it is surprising, even anxiety-arousing: "Is this the beginning? Am I starting to get turned off?" Many men and women with fairly good self-esteem and an understanding of the normal waxing and waning of desire are not disturbed by this occurrence. But it does plant in our minds the realization that we will not always desire our loved one as we did in the beginning, that our reservoirs of lust and passion are not bottomless.

When we marry, the process of getting to know each other and discovering irritating qualities in our mate has a very definite effect on how sexy we may feel. As our expectations clash and we become slightly disillusioned with the relationship, the urge to move closer and to make love is affected. We come to feel more cautious, wary at times, even mistrustful. In that atmosphere, subtle resentments and anger begin to form scar tissue that inevitably numbs our sexual responses. We start to feel disinterested.

As normal hassles and arguments become part of the marriage atmosphere, couples more often find themselves disinclined to make love. They may even view each other as less attractive or desirable. When we are not happy with someone, he or she doesn't look very appealing to us. Conversely, warm and loving feelings tend to evolve into more erotic urges and we become very receptive to our mate's overtures.

We have previously discussed the idea of dormant love, of sealing ourselves off from caring as a means of protecting ourselves from hurt and disappointment. Just as love can go underground, so too can sexual desire, and even more easily. Most of us have to feel good about our mate to want to make love; feeling neutral is not enough for many people. So when there are negative energies flowing back and forth, sexual desire can very easily be depressed. Inhibited sexual desire, then, serves as a protective mechanism. We withdraw our sexual interest because we know that during sex we will feel vulnerable, and that is too frightening.

This entire process has a spiraling effect over time. As the frequency of sexual overtures and contact diminishes, we become shy and nervous about our disinterest, and may even feel inadequate. Not everyone can maintain desire when there are difficulties in a marriage. At these times we may even fantasize about other partners. As sexual contact with our partner decreases we may, after a time, not even feel any sexual stirrings. Although we would like to be closer and to engage in some form of physical and sexual contact, the prospect is scary, because we are taking the chance that we won't become involved.

The wish for sexual contact is a result of habit more than actual physiological drive. The more you have sex, the more you want it. For many couples, the solution to inhibited sexual desire is forcing themselves to make contact again.

After a while, what seemed forced in the beginning becomes spontaneous and alive.

Tony and Deborah had been married for thirteen years. During the first five years they had had a relatively active and mutually satisfying sexual relationship. It had slowed down during the next five, and in the past three years had trailed off from once a week to once a month. Both Tony and Deborah worked hard at their jobs, and they had two children, who also demanded time and attention, which was given freely and lovingly. Prior to entering marriage counseling, the two of them would occasionally joke about their diminished sex drives, and they made a few attempts to get away for weekends partly in order to enliven this part of their marriage. Unlike so many couples who seek marriage or sex therapy because one person is much more interested in sex than the other, Tony and Deborah were equally disinterested and, as they acknowledged later in therapy, not all that upset about it.

What is often lost in a marriage is the feeling that our partner understands and is sensitive to the little things that hurt us but that may seem too trivial or even pointless to mention. It is the slow buildup of this emotional debris that creates distance and a deadening sort of discouragement. In counseling, Tony and Deborah began telling each other about these long-hidden and neglected feelings.

In the course of counseling, Tony discovered

that his particular resistance stemmed from an anxiety about recognizing just how estranged he had become from Deborah. Regardless of his conscious thoughts about sexual activity, making love was uncomfortable because it was precisely at those times that he would be aware of how little he felt for her. His love had become dormant enough that the only thing left was the friendship.

She had similar concerns. She acknowledged feeling shy with him. The easy part for the two of them was reviving the habit of sex, the purely physical appetite. Within a month, they were making love again, but being close and intimate took longer. They became aware of small resentments that had been tucked away for years— financial disputes, quarrels about the children, fights regarding social plans, all the accumulated tensions present in any marriage. Fortunately, they were able finally to clear the air, which enabled them to continue working on revitalizing their neglected erotic desires.

If disinterest gets out of hand, it creates a ripple effect, and other anxieties surrounding sex get into play. We are shy about initiating sex because it's been too long. There is the feeling that our mate won't believe our overture or will even laugh at us. Couples who have not had sex for long periods always encounter a particular roadblock in sex or marriage therapy.

Couples who suffer from disinterest are allowing themselves to be made miserable by the false belief that loving couples inevitably feel sexually drawn to each other. Not so. No amount of love necessarily overcomes the enormous shyness, inhibition, and anxiety that can be stirred by sexuality.

WHERE DID SEXUAL CHEMISTRY GO?

In addition to the serious problem of inhibited sexual desire, there is a more general sexual sluggishness that is very common today. It is as though most men and women were operating on very weak batteries, producing only the most feeble of sexual sparks. Indeed, men and women today are undoubtedly much more turned off than any of them would acknowledge. There are a number of reasons for this.

For one, the media have flooded us for years with images of sexuality and standards of performance. It is safe to say that we have become saturated with the importance of sexuality to the point that men and women are more than a little jaded. The effect of this saturation has been to desexualize us in subtle but powerful ways. There is no longer any of the delightful mystique present in sexuality that existed years ago. It is very difficult to find anything new and tantalizing. We've seen it all.

So what happens to sexual drive? If it is true that we are satiated with sexual imagery, does our drive remain blocked, does it just trickle off and die? Not at all. For some people, it remains alive, but it becomes sublimated, the energy channeled into a different, less threatening direction. The new outlet today for sexual libido seems to be work and the drive for financial security and affluence. Increasingly inhibited sexual desire in young professional people who are obsessed with their careers is no accident. Their lust is for money rather than sexual conquests or experiences.

Another way we deal with sexual satiation is by satisfying ourselves with vicarious experiences. These allow us to feel some sexual release without dealing with the underlying complex issues of sex and its relationship to love. Erotic films and magazines are still popular because they are safer than real life. You don't have to relate to anyone, you don't have to perform, and you won't be in danger of contracting a sexually transmitted disease.

Another reason for diminished sexual sparks is that in recent years there has been a deemphasis on the differences between men and women. Such differences were seen as a contributing factor in discrimination against women and stereotypical characterizations of them. But men and women are different—quite different. Trying to make them more similar may be well-meaning but is ultimately foolish and misguided. Because of attempts to make men more "feminine" and women more "masculine" there has been a blurring of distinction between the sexes and, more troublesome, a dilution of what it means to be a man or a woman. The days when a reasonably attractive man or woman could count on automatically being "noticed" by members of the opposite sex are gone. In a sense, there has been a kind of weakening of male and female sexual energy and drive as a result of this blurring. The more we are not supposed to view each other as sex objects, the less likely we are to feel sexual attraction and chemistry.

We are certainly not suggesting you view your mate as an "object," but it does help to acknowledge him or her as a sexual "being." It is only when we sense the other person's sexuality that we are attracted and want to make love.

A third reason for weak sexual chemistry between men and women today is the lingering effect of the sexual revolution. Specifically, we are referring to all of the performance demands it created in men as well as women. At its height, the sexual revolution not only liberated sexual desires and activities, it also implicitly suggested that if you weren't exploring and "realizing" your own sexual potential, you were somehow deficient and inadequate. This, along with women becoming more sexually assertive, meant men had to learn to be more skilled and sensitive lovers, which created a level of performance anxiety that we still cope with today.

As anyone reading this is well aware, men reacted to these new pressures with a variety of responses, most of them negative. There was the "new impotence"—men became so anxious about performing well and helping a woman reach orgasm that they began experiencing difficulties in getting and maintaining an erection. Of course the more anxious they became, the worse it got. Some men have become timid about initiating sex, and for some there is an undercurrent of resentment that also results in diminished interest or desire.

Women also experienced their own form of performance anxiety. Having discovered they could be more orgasmic, even have multiple orgasms provided their partner had the staying power, women felt they had to have orgasms as often as they could. However, there is a significant percentage of women who, for a variety of reasons, don't have orgasm, or can't while having conventional intercourse. For this group of women there is the pressure of having to be sexually satisfied. Not only do these women feel they should have orgasms for themselves, but they feel a need to reach a climax for the man's sake, to affirm that he is a good lover. A new kind of "orgasm anxiety" has developed for women as a result.

In addition to the specific performance anxieties suffered by men and women, there is also an overall pressure to consider frequency of sexual contact a valid measure of sexual self-esteem and marital happiness. However, studies show that while quality and quantity of sex are important in a marriage, they are by no means the critical indicator of how fulfilled a husband or wife may be.

All of these pressures contribute to the sexual confusion, frustration, and disinterest that occur in marriages today. It is important to understand these forces, for they have influenced all of us.

OVERCOMING BLAME

Whenever we feel troubled or disinterested in sex, we almost reflexively assume it is our mate's fault. From our first experience with sex we learn that sexual arousal is the result of someone stimulating us. The trigger is presumed to exist within the other person; it is the other person who has the power to make us feel sexy. The truth, of course, is almost the opposite. We are the ones who must first be receptive to sexual stimuli; we allow ourselves to be turned on or off.

In marriage, whether we are the one who feels sexually disinterested or our spouse is, we begin to blame our spouse. Even when we secretly feel ashamed about our lack of interest and therefore feel somewhat responsible, there still is the tendency to see our mate as someone who should be able to help us. This unfortunate shifting of responsibility is aided by the

erroneous beliefs and myths about marriage that
so many of us harbor.

Myth #1
Sex is a measure of love.

Many couples falsely assume that their sex life
is a measure of how much they care for each
other. The truth is that one can be deeply in
love and still have conflicts and inhibitions about
sexual expression. Sex is often an expression of
love. But when it doesn't happen, it does not
therefore follow that husband and wife are not
in love.

Another reason why sex should not and cannot be the primary measure of marital happiness is that some men and women may love
each other and marry, and yet not be very com-
patible sexually. A person who desires sex three
or four times a week may marry someone who
is quite happy with sexual activity once every
two weeks. While such mismatched couples do
have a dilemma that must be dealt with, that
does not mean they are doomed to frustration
and unhappiness. Too much publicity has been
given to sexual fulfillment without enough talk
about the range of different sexual appetites.
We are not all equal, and those with a more
modest appetite should not be made to feel
there is something wrong with them.

Bernie, age 27, had been married to Eleanor
for three years. Their marriage had been enjoy-

able and definitely met most of their expectations except in one critical area, sex. When they made love, it was pleasurable and mutually satisfying, but Eleanor typically was more romantic and liked to initiate sex more often than her husband. If she had had her way, they would have been making love at least three times a week. Bernie, on the other hand, would have been quite satisfied with once a week. Since they had been married, there had been numerous discussions about this topic. These "debates," as Bernie characterized them, were not acrimonious but never resulted in a resolution of the problem either. What had happened was typical when this kind of imbalance occurs in a marriage. Eleanor had become increasingly frustrated while Bernie had become resentful and was slowly finding her less and less desirable.

When they first sought therapy, it became clear that not only was Eleanor's drive and desire stronger than Bernie's, but Eleanor imbued the frequency of sex with significant meaning. When they made love frequently, she felt better about herself, more desirable and more loved. He, on the other hand, recognized that her requests had little to do with sexual satisfaction and more to do with validating her sense of attractiveness. He had come to feel that he was only an instrument for her self-worth. They are continuing to work on this issue, hoping to arrive at a point where they can each take responsibility for their own self-esteem. In order to be mutually satisfying on its own terms, sex has to be free from excessive emotional needs.

Myth #2
A couple's sexual feelings should match.

Another false belief about marital sex is that happy couples are somehow "in sync" most of the time, magically mirroring each other's wishes and desires. When one partner wants sex, the other is also presumed to be in the mood. We know this isn't the case, yet husbands and wives continue to blame each other for differences in their sexual urges. In fact, there are probably more ways in which couples are out of sync than in sync. They do not necessarily have major disagreements about when, where, and how, but they do have scores of minor ones. For example, women typically want sex to occur in a romantic context, when they are feeling intimate and excited to be with their husband. Men, however, are often much less concerned with intimate feelings than they are with more erotic ones. Moreover, men like a more relaxed, nonpressured atmosphere to prevail—not one fraught with meaning.

Max, 37, and Cynthia, 36, have been married for fourteen years. In all that time, they have fought over sexual issues. He insists on having sex when he is in the mood and still hasn't gotten the message that "mood" means something different for her. For him, the signal for sexual activity is a rather primitive feeling of lust that may be fairly independent of what else is going on between the two of them. Cynthia, however, is only in the mood when she is feeling intimate with Max. No matter how skilled his attempts at foreplay, if they are not feeling particularly close and warm with each other, she is not interested. He insists that marital sex often is independent of romance and intimacy. She agrees intellectually, but in her heart she feels used if sexual activity is devoid of the feelings of warmth and closeness that are so important to her. The two of them reflect an age-old, very common problem in marriage: men tend to regard sex as leading to intimacy, and women see it as the result of intimacy.

Solutions to this classic male/female dilemma are usually arrived at only after couples realize that no one is right or wrong, no one is inadequate. Once they can accept the fact that their differences are valid and that their spouse is not rejecting or punishing them, more harmonious sexual rhythms are not that difficult to establish.

When husbands or wives foolishly believe their mate should feel as they do, they then launch themselves on a campaign of change and coercion. Even though the campaign may be disguised by a light manner, these attempts at shaping their mate's personality are typically met with resentment and stir up underlying feelings of guilt and inadequacy. When we have such negative feelings, the first thing we want to avoid is having sex with the person who has made us feel that way. Differences in sexual wishes should be a signal for acceptance, understanding, and gentle communication if any. There is a rule of thumb with respect to any kind of attempted behavior change: you cannot go faster than the rate at which the other person can comfortably move. When it comes to sex in particular, you can't move faster than the slower partner. To try is to instill tension and anxiety, and it is only when we are relaxed that we are open to taking new risks in the sexual area.

Yolanda and Richard have been married for twenty-four years. For the duration of their marriage, Yolanda has felt sexually inadequate, because she has difficulty reaching orgasm. She must be very relaxed and needs a great deal of foreplay for quite a long time. The time required seems an eternity to her husband. Again, this is rather common in marriage and should not be cause for alarm and arguments, provided both husband and wife are understanding and accepting. In this case they were not. Richard feels he understands, but nevertheless criticizes her and continues to register impatience at the "task" before him. In counseling, it has been pointed out to him that she will never develop a faster response until he truly accepts the differences in their rate of response.

Sounds simple, but the fact is that Richard always has secretly regarded her behavior as a measure of his lovemaking skills. He has never felt comfortable accepting the reality of their differences.

Myth #3
Communication is the solution to sexual problems.

This is another of the widely accepted myths about marriage. If only it were as easy as merely talking to each other. If the communication were that honest, tender, and skillful, there wouldn't be difficulties in the first place. The reality is that most communication about sexual concerns is usually a conduit for blame and guilt. Imagine what happens when one person talks to another about sexual dissatisfaction. The one being talked to feels immediate criticism. The one complaining feels he or she is right because society tells us a healthy person is supposed to enjoy sex, and as often as possible. From the inception of this dialogue, real communication doesn't have a chance. The one who has to listen feels sad, angry, anxious, inadequate, and estranged.

Regardless of the specific sexual dilemma you may be encountering in your marriage, there are some general suggestions which, if heeded, will be of enormous help. Keep in mind our overall point of view—that changes in marriage are probably most effective when each person takes responsibility.

Developing a Fresh Perspective

When there is disinterest in a marriage and there are diminished expressions of desire by either partner, an atmosphere of asexuality, numbness, and at best platonic friendship prevails. The first step toward allowing something new to happen is to view your mate as a sexual being.

A brief aside is needed here for those of you who feel you are with a mate who is disinterested and you are the one who apparently has the healthy desire. Disinterest on the other person's part actually stimulates interest in a kind of perverse way. An example is the marriage in which one partner typically refuses sex and the other responds by wanting sex even more. When we want something we can't have, we often move in either of two directions: either we turn off to the point where desire is so muted that it is nonexistent, or we create an even more powerful yearning for the impossible.

Viewing your mate as a sexual being is difficult when you have been sealing yourself off to avert hurt and disappointment. After difficulties and tortured communications, married individuals find themselves looking at their mate as a source of pain rather than pleasure. It is no wonder the first sexual casualty is arousal.

What does this mean, to regard your mate as a sexual being? Remember back to the time when you really felt turned on, when you wanted your spouse regardless of the particular mood you were in? It is possible to feel that again. Underneath the layers of frustration, resentment, and negative familiarity you may be feeling now, this may seem impossible. Even so, the first step is still to take on faith the idea that you can retrieve some of those feelings. No matter what has happened, we believe that loving feelings never really die; they become dormant or are suppressed. Their potential to arouse you is still there.

Anger and resentment must be set aside if there is to be any real possibility for success in reviving dormant attraction for one another. This may sound like a "Catch-22." You may wonder, "How can I set anger aside when that is the very thing that ruined our sex life?" If you want to change your sexual relationship, you have to take responsibility for what *you* can do. Moreover, if you are making love with more desire, pleasure, and tenderness, you might find yourself more willing to get over fights without trying to prove you are right. In other words, you might find yourself enjoying more good times, and you won't want to ruin them with repetitive battles and illusory victories. The important point is consciously letting old anger go, for that is the only way you can experience a renewal of sexual feelings.

Next, reacquaint yourself with the concept that sex is, among other things, a habit. Like all habits, sexual behavior, once expressed, is more likely to be expressed again. The more often you have sexual encounters with your mate, the more likely it is that you will want to do it again.

The truth is that most couples who have some sexual difficulties in their relationship develop a secret pessimism that the spark will never return. That simply is not true, but the fear is understandable. Nothing feels worse than being cold and unresponsive to your mate's overtures. You sincerely believe you will never again feel the yearning and heat of sexual desire. Lust seems far in the distant past. But when the spark is reignited, it's just like old times. And plenty of couples have experienced just this kind of turnabout. Again, the underlying principle is a psychological one. Habits die slowly, and anything, however contrived, that restimulates what we once felt will make it more likely that we'll feel the same way again.

Overcoming Shyness

Most people suffer from varying degrees of shyness, and this is especially true when it comes to sexual behavior. No matter how much we may love our mates and be loved in return, there is still the possibility of shyness when we are in our bedrooms. Even after years of marriage, the vast majority of couples will have significant areas of reticence about their sexual relationship. This is not necessarily bad, it's just human. Were we to be totally open and expressive about our sexuality, we might even be less intrigued by the subject.

But too much shyness and emotional guardedness is detrimental to a fuller realization of what you might experience with your spouse. Sexual interest and passion are ultimately about being freer and more alive. Being passionate is a way of responding to life around us, it doesn't just mean being sexy. However, the older we get, the more difficult it is to be expressive and free. We tend to become more conservative and less spontaneous in our behavior with the passage of time. We are more reluctant to let go of inhibitions and constraints.

Taken to extremes, sexual shyness is the fear that if we let go we will be criticized, ridiculed, even disdained. To avert these possible disasters, we stubbornly and foolishly cling to our various ways of disguising what we feel.

Overcoming shyness is relatively straightforward. You must take the emotional risk, you must see yourself as capable of being more than you presently are, you must be able to see yourself doing things that you typically regard as "not me." Now, of course this is not so easy, but most people who choose to grapple with their sexual shyness and try something new discover an immediate positive payoff; instead of feeling horribly embarrassed, they find themselves experiencing more pleasure.

The most successful sex therapies today are largely based on the notion of overcoming shyness and inhibitions. Their aim is to make men and women feel more relaxed, thus allowing sexual arousal to occur. Physical sensations are muted or even numbed by anxiety. Sex therapists, in order to help couples rediscover sensuality and arousal, help them take small but significant steps that lead to a freeing of feelings. For example, instead of focusing on actual genital contact and sexual intercourse, most of the training focuses on touching and cuddling, which eventually lead to sexual arousal as the couple learn to be less shy and more relaxed.

Finally, to the degree that sexual disinterest has resulted from men's and women's loss of touch with what is essentially "feminine" or "masculine" during the last two decades, then our shyness must be conquered in order to retrieve those primitive and essential energies. Men who are freer are inherently more "manly," and women who are freer are inherently more "womanly."

Breaking Old Patterns

There is a concept in behavioral therapies called *disinhibiting stimulus* which refers to any situation or event or setting that is new or novel enough to break an existing pattern. For example, when couples go off on a vacation they often find themselves feeling revitalized in general, and more desirous of sex in particular. The reason this occurs is that in the new setting, there is a breaking of old familiar response patterns. The wish to make love is not merely a result of escaping pressures and feeling more relaxed. It is a result of seeing one's mate in a new perspective. Obviously, however, you cannot wait for vacation times to enliven your sexual life. You must involve yourself and your mate in new situations on a regular basis at home.

In marriage therapy, when couples report enjoyable sexual relations, invariably we hear that they followed an evening out or something done out of the regular routine. Again, disinhibiting stimuli were at work. The lesson here is fairly clear: if nothing new is happening, then sexual behavior is also likely to become stale and familiar.

Separateness also enhances sexual desire, because it too provides a break in typical patterns in marriage. Couples who spend some time apart, in the evening, for example, report feeling more interested in and intrigued by their mates.

Greg has been married to Nina for eight years. Recently she has become friendly with a group of women who get together to discuss novels once a week. She and Greg had a rather old-fashioned, conventional marriage and were always at home together in the evenings. When she first told Greg of her new interest, he admittedly felt a bit neglected. However, his initial reaction quickly changed. "When Nina comes home now, she seems more alive, more involved, and, to be frank, more appealing sexually. It's not that she's changed in any way, or looks different or anything like that. But she's somehow more exciting, almost like a date!" Greg has discovered how pattern-breaking sets off a whole new chain of responses. It's similar to suddenly finding you cannot take your mate for granted. Whenever husbands and wives feel some jealousy as a result of attention being paid to their mate, there is this kind of reaction. They find themselves looking at their spouse in a fresh and inviting new way.

Seducing Your Mate

When a husband or wife feels deprived or frustrated sexually, we have often posed the question, what would you do if you set out to seduce your mate? In other words, instead of complaining, what can you do on your own that might engage your mate? Most people initially find the question silly and then cite examples of verbally initiating talk of sex or perhaps trying to set up an evening which might result in a sexual encounter at its conclusion. That's not what we meant by the question. Stimulating sexual interest is not about "propositioning" your spouse, rather it is about charming, winning over, and seducing. It is an approach that takes weeks and months, not days. When people object to the task, we remind them that they are going to be married for years and this investment of time and energy is bound to pay off. When men and women begin to take a genuine interest in their spouse and give unselfishly in terms of going places and doing things, then trust is reestablished and sexual interest becomes reawakened.

A useful attitude or "mindset" is thinking about your mate as though you were courting him or her again. Take a fresh look at who your mate is, what he or she is like, how he or she responds, and make sure your perception is communicated by words and by deeds. A "second honeymoon" is in many ways exactly what we're suggesting.

After twenty-three years of marriage, Robert decided to do something about the waning frequency of sexual activity in his marriage. He began to buy tickets for concerts for the two of them to attend alone rather than with other couples. They went to restaurants that were more lively than they would ordinarily frequent with their friends, and he bought his wife a dress that was sexier than dresses she had been wearing in recent years. The result? Robert and his wife began to respond to each other in ways that had long been forgotten.

If there is one theme we wish to underscore,

it is that sexual disinterest is a normal part of many marriages, and blame is not a productive antidote. Instead, as with so many other marital dilemmas, change occurs when one or both parties have the courage to break patterns on their own, shake up the marriage system, and then come together in a new way. Becoming Self-Directed in marriage is what enables a husband or wife to take stock, put desires into action, and reawaken sexual interest. There is really no such thing as recapturing the past, but we can assume the personal responsibility for creating a fresh present that includes warm, intimate sexual expression.

CHAPTER EIGHT

When Husbands and Wives Become Friends

*I*f there is one prevailing wish that husbands and wives have, it is to be friends and close companions for life. Any survey of long-lasting and fulfilling marriages reveals that the central component that carries a couple through the tough times and allows them to benefit the most from the good ones is friendship. That being the case, one would think that we would be more aware of the ways in which we could foster this critical bond, but we aren't. In general, men and women who are about to marry know very little about how to sustain a marriage. They understand that the feeling of love is an essential marital adhesive, but often don't realize that love, in the absence of friendship, is only a hormonal illusion. One cannot desire another person over the long haul without really being friends with him or her.

It also seems we should be closer than ever to becoming true friends with our mates because of all the social upheavals in the last decade or so that have resulted in more equality between the sexes and a deemphasis on gender differences. Unfortunately, this has not been the case. Rather than more harmony, in many marriages we see a clash of expectations creating more mistrust, often leading to subtle forms of estrangement rather than friendship.

Interestingly enough, younger people may be the beneficiaries of some of the positive fallout of these social changes. Teenagers and college students do report feeling less burdened by sex-role stereotypes. Older men and women, however, are not so favorably affected.

In a superficial sense, friendship seems to be on the rise between single men and women. The blurring of sex-role definitions and the specter of AIDS have had a positive by-product—friendship has become a priority before any sexual involvement. Platonic involvement is more popular than ever before, and while some consider it less than desirable, it does provide new opportunities for men and women to learn how to become friends.

Perhaps in time, the enlightenment among young people and singles will have a "trickle-up" effect. As these young men and women marry, they will bring their knowledge of how to form friendships with one another into marriage. But for now, there are millions of husbands and wives who have yet to discover how to be close in this fashion. And, as always, there are those cynical front-line reporters on the battle of the sexes who honestly believe that men and women are so inherently different that the concept of friendship in marriage is really a delusion. Obviously, we do not find ourselves in that gloomy camp.

THE ESSENCE OF FRIENDSHIP

The poet John Donne said it most succinctly: "No man is an island." Friendship is the antidote to the dilemma we all face at one time or another in our lives—loneliness. Getting married doesn't mean we will never experience loneliness, but it does diminish our sense of separateness.

All friendships share certain qualities. First of all, there is a sense of trust. We believe a friend cares about us—we feel liked, even cherished, for who we are and what we are able and willing to give to our friend. There is a sharing of common interests and values. There is a sense of goodwill and fidelity—we believe the other person has our best interests at heart, will not betray us, and is a loyal ally.

As the friendship endures, it is strengthened by the knowledge that we have so much invested and it has rewarded us. There is also the joy of shared history, of nostalgic reminiscences about our experiences together. The future is also part of each friendship—plans, dreams, and the comfort of knowing our friend will be there to share those unfolding events with us as well.

The expression "my best friend" starts out in childhood and holds special meaning. Sadly, as we grow up, our skills at establishing these critical relationships are not as polished. Many adults are wise enough to retain old friends but terribly clumsy at making new ones. As we get older, we unfortunately develop more false pride. We become more guarded, less receptive, even though our need for such close ties has not diminished.

As adults, most of us do manage to stick our necks out enough now and again to form new friendships. We learn the complexities as well as the rewards that are involved. Adult friends are expected to make demands on each other in times of difficulty. We need them then. By their presence, they let us know we are cared about, loved. They always know when we are hurting, often merely by the sound of our voice.

Friendships can also get rocky. We may argue, offend each other, let each other down, have falling-outs, even go through times when, busy with other people or endeavors, we are in less frequent or no contact. Yet there is still the feeling we will one day reconnect, because otherwise we lose too much. Indeed, as we grow older, the value of longtime friendships is heightened. We're actually aware that it is too late to develop the deep, knowing, and sustaining ties that can only be formed by years, even decades, of sharing life's sorrows and joys.

Friendship between husbands and wives is similar to other kinds of friendships, yet it can be even deeper and more meaningful because of the added experiences of day-to-day living coupled with the complex element of sexual bonding. The essence of successful friendships between husbands and wives is the capacity to blend sexuality and passion with feelings of tenderness and companionship—often a difficult task. Nevertheless, men and women marry in order to realize that very integration of wishes. We still have the notion of our mate as friend and lover as the ideal. So, if we all crave this friend/lover quality in our mate, why then is it so difficult to realize?

UNCONSCIOUS FEARS
OF FRIENDSHIP

From the time we are young, we are all aware of the value of friendship. It is a reliable hedge against loneliness, a way to measure self-worth, and a gauge of our impact on others. Friendship is our first real experience of feeling important and connected to another person without necessarily being dependent upon him or her. Friends cherish their sense of equality, and the bond of mutual trust that develops encourages free expression. It's not that our friendships exist in some rarified atmosphere devoid of conflict—we are simply more accepting of these limitations.

Friendship is thus generally rewarding. But most couples are not aware of the resistance they have toward letting down certain critical barriers which would allow a deeper friendship between them to develop. In fact, the notion of resistance may sound a bit absurd. We don't work against friendship in other areas of our lives, so why would we within the context of marriage? The source of this unconscious resistance toward marital friendship is twofold:

1. *SELFISHNESS.* Many married couples are far more selfish with each other than they realize—more selfish than they are with their friends. They are certainly often more generous of themselves with friends than with their mate. People extend themselves to friends, they look for areas of common interest, and they put energy into being attentive to the events that go on in their friends' lives. With one's marriage partner, it is so often a different story.

It is astounding how many married couples lament not feeling closer to each other and having playful interaction and camaraderie with each other, and yet are unwilling to do anything to promote these things. When we ask, "How often do you do some of the things your mate particularly enjoys?" many people respond by saying something like "I don't like doing any of those things, and I don't do things I don't like." Friendship is a by-product of shared experiences, and a "me first" attitude prevents it from flowering.

Generosity promotes friendship; excessive and unrealistic expectations deplete it. We often approach our mate with such strong security needs that the net impact is more often one of demanding rather than giving and caring. We expect friends to enjoy us, not complete us, and we don't expect to be at the center of their lives. Friendships grow out of freedom, not guilt.

2. *SEX-ROLE STEREOTYPES.* We all are burdened to some extent by culturally conditioned gender stereotypes. These stereotypes get in the way of friendship, for feeling constrained to play out a role reduces spontaneity and the comfort and naturalness of friendship.

If these gender roles are really such a burden, why then do we tend to refuse to let them go? In many of us, there is an unconscious fear that abandoning these restrictive roles will result in our being less attracted to our partner and our partner's being, in turn, less attracted to us.

Most men, as much as they would

dearly love to free themselves, are reluctant to give up traditional gender roles for fear of being seen as less masculine and self-reliant. They also have a fear that if they acknowledge their enjoyment of their wife's strength she will become less feminine in their eyes.

Women are also restrained by the powerful tug of gender roles. Many women, despite their conscious wish for a man to be more open and expressive, harbor an unconscious fear that their husband will become too needy or emotionally dependent upon them. With regard to their own behavior, many women continue to hide their true strengths from their husbands because they are afraid of being seen as unfeminine.

When these unconscious fears are allowed to affect a relationship, they can destroy friendship. It is only when we are truly ourselves, with all of our strengths as well as weaknesses, that friendship can flourish.

BARRIERS TO FRIENDSHIP

Every relationship between a husband and wife has the potential for conflict. Just because we sign a marriage contract doesn't mean that we are now immune to the tensions that always exist between men and women.

The first barrier to friendship in a marriage is romance. Sounds odd, but it is true. Romance, intense as it may be, allows little room for the darker side of life: fears, anxieties, worries. But it is exactly these more nakedly human and compelling feelings that draw friends to one another. The sense of someone's being there for you through good times and bad is essential for a friendship. But during the romantic phase of a relationship, feelings of excitement, bliss, and ecstasy dominate instead. Yet it is the expression and sharing of our fears and concerns that makes genuine and mature intimacy, so necessary for a relationship to endure, possible. Romance talks about love; friendship puts it to the ultimate test.

Janice, married three years, is troubled over her parents' relationship. The only time she can really talk to Richie, her husband, is when they have a large block of time to themselves. "But that's exactly the time when he wants to act as if we're on a second honeymoon. It's always let's be up, let's have fun, let's not talk about anything heavy. I'm worried sick about my father's drinking, but I don't feel I can talk about it with Richie, and that makes me feel distant from him." Richie is not only being insensitive, he's damaging their marriage by preventing real closeness and friendship. What Janice needs to tell Richie is: "I understand how important it is for you to feel light and relaxed when we finally get some time to spend together. But right now, I'm afraid my father is in real trouble and I'm not sure what I can do about it. I feel like some sort of dark cloud when I get the feeling you don't want me to bring up anything that isn't fun and pleasant. I need to be able to talk to you not only about what makes me feel good, but also about the things that worry me and make me feel bad. This is one of those times. I want to talk to you about my father." Being direct and honest about how she feels while at the same time acknowledging Richie's discomfort with sad or worrisome feelings can lead to more open, fulfilling, and textured communication.

Oddly enough, a major reason why husbands and wives are not more companionable is that they unconsciously assume a mate is something different from a friend. Such individuals may describe their partner as a lover, a person they adore, or a mate toward whom they have fierce protective feelings, but what is often left out is the notion of a mate as a peer, a friend, a pal. It is almost as though such individuals have an antique view of marriage as the meshing of functions and needs but not friendship. They look outside the marriage for something as simple and everyday as a friend.

Adrienne has been married for seventeen years. In her view she has a good marriage, but one that is not very intimate. She grew up in a home of hardworking parents who rarely spoke to each other except about the children. Adrienne admits, "I really see Bill as a provider, as the spine of this family, and yet I find myself

seeking out my women friends when I need to
talk about problems other than our daughter."
Adrienne assumes her husband is the key person in her life, but his presence is more symbolic than real. She cannot conceive of her
husband's being her good friend, and frankly
has never tested this possibility.

Obviously, the most common barrier to becoming a friend to your spouse is regarding the
other person as an enemy. There are fights and
arguments in every marriage, but contrary to
popular belief, most marital conflicts are not
fully resolved. They usually get set aside in a
kind of uneasy truce, the underlying feelings
shoved into the background. When enough anger and resentment have slowly accumulated,
most couples cannot even conceive of a genuine
friendship based on liking and mutual enjoyment.

Garrett, married for six years, smiles ruefully
when asked about friendship. "I'm happy when
we go out and have a good time with other
couples and don't fight about all the garbage
we usually battle about. Talking about friendship sounds like a *Reader's Digest* article to me."
Beneath that cynicism is a lot of sadness, for
Garrett, like all of us, had hoped for more in his
marriage. He has almost given up on what may
be the ultimate reward in a relationship, and
his wife is equally disappointed. The two of
them feel there is nothing they can do to change
things.

Friendship between husbands and wives is
often hindered by the presence of misunder-

standings based on fallacious thinking. Specifically, the myths about marriage we have already explored add to the difficulty of establishing friendship with our mate. Because of our deep-seated fantasies and wishes about marriage, we tend to confuse expectations about love and romance with the more reasonable expectations about what a friend means in the context of marriage.

For example, the possibility of friendship occurs only when we approach our mates as equals. Yet we are often so hungry for approval in order to feel worthwhile and complete that we may view our spouse as a solution to our inadequacies. Rather than looking for the give-and-take of an equal relationship, we may impose unrealistic expectations upon our mates which work against ever becoming friends.

John, married twelve years, insists that Catherine, his wife, is not as good a friend as he would like her to be. Although he looks to his wife for an inordinate amount of approval and praise, partly because of her savvy and intelligence, which drew him to her in the first place, whenever she gives him any critical comments he tunes out and walks away. Clearly, friends are able to give each other honest feedback—indeed, that is one of their greatest values. By not allowing this from his wife, John is shutting off communication and preventing a friendship from blossoming. He really wants a mother figure who gives unconditional love and praise. What he needs is an honest friend.

A common barrier to friendship occurs when we confuse friendship rights with marital rights. As husbands and wives, we feel we can make demands on our mate to change this or that trait. At the same time, we want our mate to be our friend, forgetting that friends do not impose such unrealistic expectations on each other. Friends are much more likely to be tolerant of differences. Friends are typically sought out based on similarities of belief and interests. They are not, however, emotionally invested in reducing or negotiating away their differences. With friends, we are not threatened by differences; we allow for their presence and let our friends be who they are. Indeed, the sense of acceptance and understanding we get out of a friendship is what makes it feel alive and comfortable. We like our friends for who they are, not for what we would like them to be. Just because we are married doesn't mean we have the license to mold our mate to our liking. Naturally, because friends are not living under the same roof day after day, it is much easier to be tolerant. Nevertheless, such acceptance is still a prerequisite for friendship.

Too often differences in marriage partners are somehow seen as threatening. It is as though these differences had to be harbingers of later dissension and even possible abandonment. But in a good friendship we support even those differences. When that occurs, friends are trusting with each other, more open.

The core element in a friendship is a basic

sense of understanding. Friends can allow themselves to disagree heatedly and still feel understood. But all too often in marriage any disagreement is interpreted as arising from a lack of understanding and acceptance. We don't expect friends to be mirror images of ourselves, but admit to it or not, many of us expect our mates to be exactly that.

In our experience, husbands and wives have greater difficulty than ever before in understanding each other. Part of the reason for this is that there are specific myths or false assumptions about the opposite sex that get in our way.

MYTHS WOMEN HAVE ABOUT MEN

Most of us are aware that women have been subjected to stereotyping, both positive and negative. But men have also been viewed through filters of prejudice, anger, and fear. Here are three of the false assumptions about men that always diminish the likelihood of being friends with them.

Myth #1
Men don't value friendships with women.

Women tend to believe that men do not truly value friendship with a woman. They believe that men prefer spending time with their "buddies" and engaging in more masculine pursuits. This is a tired old stereotype that has been perpetuated for generations.

In the old days, the idea that men and women could be friends simply wasn't something we could accept. A commonly held belief was that men and women were so different and had such divergent values and ideas that they could never get along. In recent years, however, there has been a dramatic and continuing evolution in sex roles and behavior. One effect of this is that men and women are much more aware of their similarities than ever before. After having gone through a long period of adversarial tension and mistrust, we are entering a new era of greater equality and respect. The more equal and the more similar our ambitions and struggles, the greater the probability we can relate to each other in the way that we do with like-sexed friends. We are discovering that while differences may enhance attraction, similarities make us feel more trusting and interested in each other.

For those women who are skeptical about achieving this kind of friendship, here's some advice. Trust that men want to be friends, and begin acting on that assumption, for you will find it works. When men are queried about friendship, perhaps the highest compliment they can pay their wife is to characterize her as their best friend. There are scores of husbands who will readily admit the only person they can rely upon is their wife, and they are deeply grateful. Husbands do wish to be friends with their wives.

As adults, it is very difficult to set up new relationships. Making friends is not easy. That is all the more reason for a man to turn to the woman in his life. And, unfortunately, if a wife believes that her husband doesn't value friendship with her, she will not expect it and not look for those signs in him that suggest that he wants it.

Myth #2
Men fear getting too close.

Some wives are pessimistic about being friends with their husband because they believe men are afraid of the intimate nature of friendship. It is true that a good friendship requires intimacy, and intimacy requires a close emotional bond that comes from mutual sharing and understanding. Intimacy also requires trust, since it involves the exposing of our most private and vulnerable feelings. Husbands and wives often confuse excessive communication with intimacy; they are not the same. You can share your innermost thoughts and feelings, but if they are not received by the other, then you are unfortunately just doing a "solo," as too often occurs in marriage.

Typically, in our society, we assume women are very comfortable being intimate and men are not. Complaints over intimacy or the lack of it are probably the most common reason couples enter marital therapy. And invariably it is the woman who initiates the contact. Men, it is commonly believed by women, have a much more difficult time expressing themselves and allowing closeness to occur. But this is a myth. Yes, it is true that men do not approach intimacy in the same way as do women, nor do men talk about their wish to be close in the same outspoken way women do, but they nevertheless want it.

Because of their deep-rooted fear of being engulfed and feminized by intense closeness, most men can allow themselves to be intimate only for much shorter periods than women. But—and we cannot emphasize this too much— this does not mean that men don't want and need closeness, because they do. Women often confuse men's discomfort with closeness with a lack of desire for it, a critical error in logic.

Men will often joke about women wanting love and romance all the time. But the truth is that deep inside, far below the level of conscious awareness, men actually may have more pent-up needs for intimacy than do women! Men's talk of sex and sexual conquest has always been a kind of disguised way of expressing their needs for emotional contact and nurturance. Women who deny or are unaware of this need in men often unknowingly neglect a man's wish for intimacy. As a result, they do not realize how alone he may feel. And, unfortunately, husbands will not talk about this deeply felt need for fear of being humiliated.

There are many disguises that a man's unrecognized and unfulfilled wish for intimacy may take in marriage. Sometimes it is expressed by his pulling away from his wife and exhibiting only a silent anger and resentment. Other men may be numbing themselves with alcohol or drugs, as a form of denial. Still other men become obsessed with physical fitness as a way of disguising emotional hungers—as though fitness could ever be a substitute for being held.

Women who believe men do not want to feel close and bonded will not be on the lookout for signs of such needs in their mate. Then the husband inadvertently confirms the wife's mistaken notion by acting as though intimacy weren't critical for him. Just realize that all of us, men and women, husbands and wives, are born with the wish to feel close and secure; none of us is comfortable feeling alone. Whenever any man looks as though he doesn't need warm, accepting contact, it is only a self-protective measure, not a wish. Men do want intimacy. Even if you don't see that need expressed by your spouse, trust that it is there but hidden.

Teasing out many a man's need for closeness requires a sensitivity to the often subtle signs of his disguised wishes. Such wishes are frequently embedded in the expression of some fanciful dream, a comment about a worrisome issue at work, a mention of doubt or feelings of insecurity, or even a request for physical contact that is out of the ordinary. All of these little signs or actions, if perceived, may be openings through which the bond of closeness can be strengthened.

Myth #3
Men don't appreciate bright and assertive women.

Whenever we attempt to explode this false belief, women invariably are skeptical. They are convinced a woman's strength is intimidating to men. Yet over and over again, in our practices and in talking to men and women at lectures and workshops, we find that men are drawn to bright and ambitious women. Then why does this myth prevail? We believe the problem lies not with a woman's strength and intelligence but with the anger and bitterness that may coexist with these qualities and make men shy away from her. Is it the anger, not the intelligence, that prompts the hasty retreat? Are anger and intelligence linked, then? Do smart and able women tend to be more angry?

At times, yes. In our work with women, we have found that many of them are unaware of this link between anger and strength. Some women are uncomfortable with their own strength, and it is their discomfort that unsettles the man. Others naively believe that if men can take wisecracks and competitiveness from another man, why can't they from a woman?

The basic premise is wrong here. When a man feels the heat of anger or the sting of criticism from another man, he feels just as wary and standoffish as he would with a woman. No one, man or woman, likes to be on the receiving end of barbs, no matter how clever.

The truth is, an increasing number of men are actually drawn to strong women, especially today when the two-career family is common. Instead of being threatened by the new career woman, men are coming to see her as a partner, a coprovider sharing the burden. Since the feminist movement, women either at work or at home are more enlightened, feel more entitled, and are more likely to drop old pseudo-feminine ways of acting. It is true that men were taken aback at first, but now men are accepting and indeed enjoying women's new strengths.

In marriages today, the woman who becomes a confidante or adviser to her husband is much more likely to have a close, intimate bond than a woman who still clings to outmoded and subservient ways of relating. Suppose you were a husband who felt hassled or overwhelmed by work issues—imagine how much more fulfilling it could be to relate to a woman who truly understood your dilemma and could be a sounding board for you. There are scores of men who will never share these concerns with other men because of shame or competitiveness. Therefore, a wife's strength and confidence become powerful assets for him.

There are still husbands who may appear to

resent assertiveness and determination in their wife, but eventually, with enough time and gentle persistence, they usually come around. Women who have spent a lot of time around men often have no difficulty with this for one simple reason: they approach men in an easy and nonthreatening way. They do not expect resistance or intimidation, and because of that they rarely encounter it.

Wives who act as though this myth were true are cheating themselves of a deeper, more equal, and more satisfying relationship with the man in their life. If a woman trusts her strength, and it accompanies her love, she has nothing to worry about. She will find her husband moving closer to her, and finally becoming a friend.

MYTHS MEN HAVE
ABOUT WOMEN

Many of the stereotypes men had about women in general and their wives in particular have been demythologized in recent years since the women's movement. But there are still two false assumptions that prevent scores of husbands from becoming friends with their wives.

Myth #1
Most women think friendship is the same as romance.

There are husbands who are convinced a wife's desire for more friendship is really a disguised way of asking for romance and intimacy. And this confusion makes men suspicious. Men who believe this are still under the impression that the quest for love and romance is the predominant concern of all women. It is not so, though the media and advertising make it seem this way. Millions of married women in this country are interested in equality and companionship in the same way that men are. This false assumption comes about, typically, because most marriages are a bit impoverished when it comes to intimacy.

Rachel, married sixteen years, finds that when she tries to get close to Alex, her husband, he immediately thinks she wants to be romantic. "He knows I do like being romantic, but I also want to be a friend to Alex. He is the one who confuses the two, and doesn't trust any suggestion I make. If I want to have a simple quiet weekend away, he thinks it means we're supposed to be gazing into each other's eyes over candlelit dinners. That's just not so." What is true with the two of them is that they keep confusing two different sets of needs. Alex needs to realize that much of Rachel's wish for closeness and interaction is a reflection of her desire for a richer friendship with him, not some devious plot to ensnare him in some cloying romantic interlude. Rachel should suggest very specific plans for a weekend outing that include a number of possible activities she and Alex could do together. Some men's discomfort with closeness and romance is elevated by vague, open-ended time spent. For such men, the more specific the plan, the greater the comfort and opportunity for warm, shared experiences.

Myth #2
Women don't like to play.

All of a man's play involves some form of competition either actively or vicariously against himself, an opponent, or even a worthy animal. Play serves two primary functions for men: it is an antidote to stress, releasing tensions and anxieties, and it is a highly symbolic way of creating challenges and proving their strength, vitality, and manhood.

Most men think women do not enjoy play. Women do like to play, but they play differently, a fact that men often don't recognize. First of all, women tend to be less competitive than men, for whom everything is a contest. Women tend not to view the contest as all that interesting. Men simply can't conceive of play unless it involves some sort of challenge or competition, while women have a broader range of activities that they experience in a playful way.

Women tend to have many more close friends

than do men, and much of what feels "playful" involves an interaction with their friends. Women, through their richer social networks, are able to release anxieties and tensions by talking. What women get out with words, men get out on the racquetball court. Women like to chat, gather in groups, and talk for hours on the phone. These activities are a kind of play that keeps them feeling connected to their friends and allows them to use these relationships as valuable sources of feedback. Men too use play as a conduit for connection to friends, but it's usually a lot easier for a man to experience the friendship through some shared event or athletic activity than it is to simply sit down and talk.

A good deal of men's play is used to shore up and reinforce a sense of identity. Competition, challenge, courage, and risk-taking are elements of men's play that make them feel more masculine. This can be experienced with intensity even when the play is a vicarious spectator sport. Picture men cheering wildly in the stands at a football game and you will understand the direct connection they have, at that moment, to the player who just scored the touchdown.

Men sometimes have a hard time seeing women as playful because they saw their mothers as being serious and no-nonsense. Generally, it is the father who is more overtly playful with a son, goofing around, teaching him how to throw a football, or wrestling and tickling in bed in the morning. It's the mother who usually gets fed up with the commotion and puts a stop to the activities. Fathers tend to encourage rough play, and mothers tend to be a bit afraid of it, fearing the boy will be hurt. Boys grow up seeing women as more cautious, conservative, and fearful about physical play.

The truth is that women enjoy playing every bit as much as men. It's just that how they express that enjoyment is different. It's a mistake for men to see women as overly serious and not needing playful outlets, for such a false assumption only creates distance rather than fostering closeness. A far more constructive path would be to find some middle ground in which play can be experienced by both the man and the woman. Interestingly, what prevents couples from playing more is not necessarily difficulty in finding common pursuits but just getting started in the first place. So often, we assume that if we love each other, play should automatically evolve. It doesn't happen that way. Husbands and wives who play well are those who sit down and explore that wish in a conscious and deliberate way. Meaningful shared activities, such as taking classes together, is something that one or both people make happen; it rarely comes about spontaneously.

PRIVACY VS. TOGETHERNESS

There are couples who work together and still want to spend all their leisure time with each other. There are others, however, who need to get away, who find themselves becoming a bit bored even though at other times they feel terrific together. There are widely varying styles and preferences, and a good marriage can take any of them into account.

The wish for privacy is one of the milestones ending the purely romantic phase of a relationship and beginning the more mature form of love. Romance is often characterized by constant togetherness and sharing. The first time we wanted to go off by ourselves to read a book or watch TV may have seemed like a violation of the romantic pact. Some men and women, when they go off like this, even wonder if their need for time alone is a sign that love is waning. Naturally, one's wish for periods of separateness has nothing to do with love or even romance. We all have our saturation point; we all need to relax and not have to perform.

Unfortunately, this need for alone time is typically not discussed in marriage, as though to mention it would suggest something is wrong. Some people naively believe that to love someone we must always enjoy spending time together. This belief is patently false. Conflict surrounding this issue often surfaces because husbands and wives are usually out of sync about being separate; one usually wants it more than the other. Usually the one who craves closeness feels more self-righteous and loving, though of course this isn't true. The person who wants privacy does so for his or her own personal needs, not out of a lack of love or a wish to pull away. For that reason, working out the timing and duration of private times can be a bit tricky. If you discuss privacy as a reasonable issue you will have a more harmonious dialogue than if you discuss it as tantamount to open marriage. The person wanting more privacy should not be made to feel guilty, yet that so often happens.

A husband or wife who wants more privacy will be effective in negotiating it as long as he or she stays positive and affirmative rather than negative and threatening. For example, if a wife wants more time with women friends, she can broach the subject by telling her husband what she enjoys about these friendships rather than inadvertently implying that she wants to get away from him. Interestingly, men have traditionally exercised this right of privacy by going off to the gym, stopping by the office on the weekend, or playing in a regular poker game, for instance. Women, on the other hand, who understandably may want some privacy too, even today often encounter subtle resistance from their husbands. But regardless of who wants it, approaching one's mate on the issue with warmth and love will usually defuse any negative response. When we feel loved and secure, we tend not to be threatened by a loved one's desire for involvements away from us.

Not everyone desires the same degree of openness. Again, differences between husbands and wives should be viewed only as that, differences rather than proofs of how loving one may be. We have already discussed the fact that one person may desire more openness than another, and such differences need to be tolerated and accepted rather than resented. Obviously, there should be reasonable bounds. It is unreasonable to expect to know our partner's every waking thought and feeling, but on the other hand it is hurtful for a partner never to want to talk about his or her concerns and reactions. A healthy sense of privacy and openness lies somewhere in between.

Our discomfort with our mate's need for privacy is often linked to feelings of possessiveness and sexual jealousy. Put simply, many husbands and wives are apprehensive about their mate's separate activities for fear their mate will meet someone new, exciting, and ultimately tempting. And this concern is not entirely groundless. Many affairs have come about solely because of proximity between a man and a woman. When they are working together or playing together, men and women become closer, more open, and more intimate with each other and may also feel the stirrings of sexual attraction. When loyalty and fidelity are tested at these times, most of us pass. When we are mature enough to know that a wish can remain just that, or a flirtation can be harmless when not acted upon, then such temptations need not be threatening to the marriage. Indeed, one can argue that not allowing room for some amount of privacy in marriage can have the effect of intensifying the need for separate experiences, including those involving the opposite sex.

Some degree of separation, rather than increasing the possibility of sexual infidelity, can stimulate greater interest and pleasure in marital sex. One cause of disinterest in a relationship is a lack of novelty and a fresh perspective. If they have time away from each other, have different experiences, men and women come back and see each other in a new light. Ironically, the more slack we give our partner, the more his or her desire for and attraction to us will be heightened.

Men and women who possess sufficient self-esteem, who feel complete and secure, find it relatively easy to accept a certain amount of separateness. Those who are not so secure, however, will find it threatening. Whenever we have difficulty being comfortable with our own independence, we tend to become suffocating with our mate. We fail to understand that it is our own problem to solve and not our mate's. The solution is to realize that private time and separateness are not fatal and that our discomfort may have less to do with love for our partner than it does with a fear of being alone. It is not fair to burden our mate with our fears of aloneness and make our mate feel responsible. He or she will invariably feel constricted and want to pull away in order to get breathing room.

BECOMING COMPANIONS

We are convinced that every marriage has the potential for satisfying levels of companionship. The couples we have studied who are most successful at creating friendship in their relationships are those who take the initiative for change. They choose to take action rather than bemoaning their fates and playing out the safe role of victim. Those husbands and wives who are caught up in deciding what is fair and reasonable have self-righteousness as their only reward.

There are couples who, when we suggest taking the initiative, may agree with our advice but are essentially pessimistic about the results. This is especially true of couples who have been married for a long time. Such couples are often so far removed from regarding each other as a potential friend they don't even know how to begin. Often the only topic of conversation that unites them is their children or grandchildren. Many of these couples are not necessarily unhappy, they just feel an all too familiar awkwardness whenever they spend too much time alone with each other. It's as though they have forgotten how to talk. Our belief is that these couples can still revitalize their relationship, but they must first acknowledge to themselves that they have to start over. Rather than bemoaning the fact that they have quietly drifted apart, they have to just accept that it happened and then face the task at hand. Couples who take the responsibility for creating new experiences often find a fresh way of seeing each other as a friend. They break patterns and avoid stagnation by creating novelty. This can be accomplished by any number of activities or interests, such as travel, classes, new friends, or even renewing old interests that have lain dormant. Discovering your marriage needs deliberate revitalization doesn't mean you have a dead marriage, it merely reveals how easy it is for all of us to drift, take each other for granted, and become stuck in old patterns.

Before any relationship can be revitalized, there must first be a clearing away of old unfinished business. In marriage, this means that old grudges and resentments have to be set aside. Note that we did not say "resolved," but "set aside." Most old conflicts will never be resolved, and efforts to resolve them are more often than not a veiled attempt to win a final victory. We just have to let go of certain conflicts and move on with our lives.

When we insist on holding on to negative feelings that block the possibility of friendship, it is not that we want to torture our spouse. Rather, we believe that these reminders of past hurts will somehow protect us from yet again being hurt in the future. We wear this armor to insulate ourselves from further disappointment. We are distrustful. The solution? When faced with such a mate, the only successful approach to regaining trust is not talk or wishful promises, no matter how well meant, but action.

Spouses who want to get close to their mate will do so only by changing their behavior, not their words. When they conduct themselves in a lively and engaging way that promises warm companionship, eventually the other person will have to respond.

Jason had been married to Lillian for twenty-eight years. In that time they had gone through good times and bad. He also had had an affair early in their marriage, which had been discovered and led to years of pain and distrust on Lillian's part. Moreover, Jason had been rather critical of her, which caused her to gradually withdraw from him. Now their children were grown and out of the house, and facing the "empty nest" made both of them a bit anxious. Even though they agreed their marriage hadn't been a perfect one, they were committed to staying together. At first Jason criticized Lillian for not being more enthusiastic when he suggested new activities, even though most of them were solely to his liking. Lillian wanted to travel in groups, and he hated that idea. Finally, with a little wisdom, Jason decided to stop negative communications and arranged for a tour to Russia, which he knew she would love. That one event proved to be a turning point for them. It was a single unselfish act that said more about his caring for his wife than any amount of talking could ever do.

There are as many styles of friendship as there are people. Husbands and wives who truly wish to keep their love alive will not try to force their mate into seeing friendship only in their own terms. We have found two basic styles which often pose the potential for disagreement: one is activity-oriented, and the other is communication-oriented. For example, the man who likes to sail may relax in a quieter nonverbal way than the woman who most prefers going to plays. One style is not inherently better than the other, and ideally we should be open to both. But if you wish to be a friend to your mate, see and appreciate what he or she likes. Do it first. Have patience—you will eventually find that your mate will reciprocate.

A final thought. In working with couples, we have found that they originally were drawn to each other because of interests or traits they found delightful but later were forgotten as the marriage progressed. Men and women who are willing to spend some time examining their past rather easily discover the path to friendship in marriage. The books you enjoyed reading together, the recreational activities that were fun before the kids arrived, the lazy Sundays at swap meets that you haven't attended for years—these are clues that can help you discover how to reconnect in new and invigorating ways. But establishing bonds of friendship is not simply a matter of looking backward and rediscovering what you enjoyed in the past. Rather, friendship requires new experiences, doing things together that create a current and evolving base of commonality.

Friendship is not a passive process. It doesn't

happen by accident, and it doesn't happen when we sit back expecting someone else either to start it or to provide the follow-through for it. Friendship is action. It requires that we be Self-Directed. It happens when we do something to encourage it, when we take a step toward our partner, when we place ourselves, for a time, within the sphere of our partner's interests and needs. Friendship is not self-involvement. It is involvement outside the confines of our singular interests and includes attending to the wishes and needs of our mate. We are all fundamentally alone in this life, but friendship reaches across the gulf allowing us to feel accepted, important, and understood.

CHAPTER NINE

Rediscovering the Family

*B*ecoming mothers and fathers as well as wives and husbands is without a doubt the most serious and meaningful joint project we will ever engage in, binding us even more closely together with shared hopes and concerns. But the innocent dreams and simple wishes we have about our family in the beginning offer no hint of the difficulty and complexity to come.

A mother: "It was all so much easier when Allison was little. I was home then and I loved the times we spent together, but these last few years since I've been back at work everything seems to have gotten so much harder. I've got so many obligations beyond the family that it's hard to take care of things. I feel torn—I like working and being out of the house, but I feel guilty for not being more available to Allison.

And I really get annoyed at Jack for not being more involved."

A father: "I don't know what's happened. I love my family, but I've gotten into such a rat race, trying to make sure we can meet our expenses every month, that even if I'm not working I'm thinking about it. I wish we'd never gotten into this two-career-family stuff—our income has gone up, but so has our spending, and more and more it feels like home is just a place where I go to refuel so I can go back to work."

A daughter: "I can remember when we used to eat supper together every night. And on Sunday mornings, I'd run and jump into bed with my mom and dad and we'd read the funnies out loud and have tickle fights. That was a long time ago. Now everything's different. We all just grab food when we're hungry, and the last time we did anything as a family was when we went to my uncle's funeral. My parents don't know where I am most of the time, and even though they sort of ask questions once in a while I don't think they care all that much. They're both real busy and gone most of the time, and it's a whole lot lonelier coming home to an empty dark house than it is being out with my friends. In a way, my friends feel more like my family than my mom and dad do."

A SHARED DILEMMA

What is happening in our families today? How do the hopes we bring to our families slip so easily through our fingertips? Long gone are the lazy summer days of Sunday barbecues and watching *Father Knows Best*. But during the past thirty years we've lost far more than our innocence. What we've lost is a good deal of our willingness to actively and responsibly shape the ongoing day-to-day experience of our families. Most of us feel vaguely out of control when it comes to our children—we see them as captives of the music they hear and the explicit films they watch, endangered by the prevalence of drugs today, the conspicuous absence of heroes, and the disrespect for authority. We so often feel the victims of social forces beyond us that we throw up our hands and redirect our attention to aspects of our own private lives we believe we can more directly control.

But the truth is that problems only seem to be "out there"—in fact, their origins are ultimately within the home, created by us! We've constructed this situation by becoming Other-Directed and unwittingly selfish and irresponsible.

Most parents feel powerless and ineffective when it comes to putting their wishes into action. They have lost touch with the real rewards of the family experience, because they've gradually reduced their active involvement with family issues to a minimum. Fulfillment doesn't come from watching, waiting, and hoping, but from participation. In the same way that the experience of love comes from active loving, the experience of family comes from active parenting.

In the beginning, many of us believed we would do better than our parents in raising a family. We saw so clearly their failures and mistakes, and we promised ourselves that we would not make those same errors. We would spend the quality time with our children we missed with our parents. We would be more sensitive and understanding. We wouldn't overlook the things our parents missed; we would be smarter. But reading bedtime stories is wearisome if you're exhausted or even impossible if you get home after the kids are asleep. And it gets tiresome having to step in to settle the same squabbles that erupt day after day. It is a constant and unrewarding challenge having to handle the willful teenager who talks back in ways we would never have dared to. And dealing with the hair, the makeup, the music, the drugs, and now AIDS is overwhelming. Sorting out their friends, knowing who is a good influence and who is not, is exhausting. Shell-shocked and battle-worn, we all too often watch helplessly as our family slowly disintegrates before our eyes. We don't step into the breach and take responsibility for this tragic erosion, but rather we place it "out there." Husbands too frequently blame their wives for not being better, more nurturing mothers, and many wives have a tendency to blame husbands for not being more active, attentive, and disciplinary fathers. In essence, we create our ongoing disappointments in our family life and then hold each other responsible.

MOTHERS AND FATHERS

One of the more obvious reasons it is harder to be a parent today is that so much more is demanded of us. Not long ago, roles were more sharply defined, and we knew what was expected. A mother's job was to prepare and manage the nest, the father's to keep it well stocked. If the mother was soothing her child over a skinned knee received from a fall from a tree, it was the father who had most likely encouraged the climb. The mother's role was to understand, nurture, and ask why, the father's to push and ask why not. The mother was the gentle hand, the father the firm boot. But during the past twenty years, we've tossed those old notions high in the air and watched them flutter slowly to the ground in all sorts of new, much more confusing patterns.

Recent social changes now demand that we each take on and master aspects of the other gender's traditional roles. As women moved into work outside the home and career development, they had to deal with and master the more aggressive aspects of their personalities. And conversely, men were expected to become more comfortable with and competent at being nurturing, tender, and empathic. Two decades into this new learning process, we have seen some interesting results. Men are participating in child care in a much broader way than ever before. And women have obviously developed competence in the marketplace. Less available working mothers have often been compensated for by more available fathers. And the added bonuses are father models that are seen as more accessible and nurturing and mother models that are seen as stronger and more competent in the arena outside the home.

"When Mary Ruth decided to go back to work, I've got to tell you I had a lot of misgivings," Jake says. "We needed money, and she really needed to work for the stimulation, too. But I worried about what effect her working would have on the kids and, frankly, how I was going to handle some of the responsibilities. It's actually worked out pretty well. I make the lunches and take my turn cooking meals and doing the clean-up details. Now I realize how much I'd come to take for granted—it's exhausting and pretty thankless. But the thing I enjoy is doing more with the kids. I've gone alone to parent-teacher conferences, I've helped them shop for clothes, I drive the carpool once a week. What's interesting is that I've gotten so much closer to the kids—we talk more, I know their friends, and I'm really on top of all the little day-to-day details in their lives. I feel more connected and more like a father than I ever did."

Rather than losing sight of the importance of

family activities, Mary Ruth and Jake have managed to retain its centrality. As she explains, "Before I started working again, I was feeling trapped and resentful. It seemed like everything I did with my children was a suffocating obligation and not much fun at all. Now that Jake has taken over some of the things that need to be done I feel so much freer. I look forward to coming home and seeing the kids, and I'm not nearly so easily annoyed as I used to be. I also think it's good for all of them—particularly the girls—to see me out there doing something besides housework. Even though it's a lot more work trying to keep everything organized, we all seem to be pretty happy."

The problem is that there still has to be a responsible caretaker regardless of who it is. As mothers have moved somewhat away from their traditional role, a gap has been created. This gap has been only partially filled by fathers expanding their participation. For the most part, fathers haven't really taken up where mothers left off, and the loser in this equation is the child.

The particular day-to-day care of children need not be the sole responsibility of either gender, but one or the other or both parents must step in and make sure the gap is filled. One father who has made a real effort in that direction proudly says, "Friends of my boys drop by even when the kids aren't home just to sit around and talk. I enjoy these kids, and I think they end up talking out with me all those things they can't seem to discuss with their own parents."

Some husbands and wives are beginning to rediscover the enormous rewards of family life. Yet impossible expectations often set them against each other. Too often, Other-Directedness tarnishes the family portrait because husbands and wives as fathers and mothers look to the other person or look outside the family for solutions to age-old conflicts. Perhaps the first step in becoming Self-Directed and rediscovering the family is to understand how each of us as a parent is shaped by the past.

ECHOES FROM THE PAST

As we leave the families of our origins and seek to create new ones of our own, we do so with the belief that we are starting anew. We do this to prove we are not simply our parents' clones, and, in part, to heal the wounds we received in our own imperfect childhoods. But the families of our past provided us with our first experiences of love and social interaction and created an indelible blueprint for how we see ourselves and care for others.

Unfortunately, our pasts are not so easy to abandon, try as we may. We are molded by our first families, and despite all our attempts at change, we mirror, more often than not, one or both parents. We seek to see our loved ones through our own eyes and to talk to them with our own voice, but it is not so easy to separate the powerful lessons we learned so long ago from our behavior today.

"I used to hate it when my father would tell me not to throw a ball in the house," recalls a young father, "so I was shocked the first time I heard those same words in the same annoyed tone of voice come out of my mouth. When I found myself putting on the same disgusted, guilt-inducing face, it was like staring at my father in the mirror." A woman exclaims, "My mother is the most critical, controlling, and self-righteous person I've ever known. When I was a kid I could never do anything right, and I promised myself that if I ever had children I would find things in them that I could encourage. I'm appalled when I find myself saying things to my kids about eating, bedtime, or studying that are word for word what my mother used to say. I thought when I left home I'd escaped her influence. It's creepy hearing her talk through my mouth."

These are not at all unusual experiences. Most of us, if we are at all attentive, are aware of the attitudes, prejudices, and idiosyncrasies of our parents that continue to influence us. We all had flawed experiences within our original families. But despite the magnitude of those imperfections, we all, at some level, unconsciously tend to re-create our own family experiences by playing out in the present these old roles and attitudes from our past. Sometimes what we do in our new family is to play out the exact opposite of our earlier experiences, giving us the illusion that we have somehow escaped the influence. But all we have really succeeded in doing is pulling the sock inside out, and we remain as bound to the past as if we behaved in exactly the same way as did our parents.

Responding in automatic, unconscious ways is often inappropriate and hurtful to our families. The only effective break with the past comes from recognizing the disguised ways these old roles and attitudes play themselves out and assuming responsibility for altering them.

Unfortunately, many of us don't do this. Rather, we inaccurately blame some of the consequences for what goes awry with our children on our mates. "He thinks I'm too affectionate with our son," laments a young mother. "I don't know, maybe I am, but I know how much attention and cuddling Charlie needs, and he doesn't get much from his father. It's not that his dad doesn't care. He's absolutely crazy about Charlie, but he has a hard time showing it." Charlie's father is a man who never received any affection from his own father, who was threatened by physical contact. The legacy of discomfort with tenderness and affection toward his son created a vacuum into which Charlie's mother was drawn. The father sees the problem as his wife's need to be overly affectionate rather than recognizing that she is in effect compensating for his emotional constriction.

If Charlie's father had the courage to see his

own difficulties with the expression of feelings, not only would his son benefit but he would too. Giving Charlie the tenderness and affection he needs would also provide the father with a vicarious way to heal his own old wounds. It is only through this sort of recognition that we can hope to free ourselves to be loving and constructive parents.

WHEN PARENTS CLASH

Most of us start our families with very little real planning or even much discussion about how children will change the relationship. Many parents, involved in their busy lives, think that having a baby is something they can do in addition to whatever else is going on; they don't realize what an incredibly demanding and exhausting job they've undertaken. Starting a family forces us to set up priorities. It makes us ask ourselves what kind of mothers and fathers we expect to be and how much of our energies we are willing to give to these new roles. Most of us make these choices in a slapdash fashion, concluding that raising a family can't be all that hard or complicated. After all, people have been having babies forever. But raising children, especially today, is a tough, complicated job, and for some very predictable reasons.

Tolerating Differences

We all have different visions of what we would like our children to be, how we want them raised, and what values we want conveyed. Many of these differences remain hidden until we start having children. It is one thing to talk in the abstract and quite another to put our words into action. Having children often brings up conflicts in people that have lain dormant because they only become relevant when a child's well-being and development are at stake.

But simply because we have different points of view doesn't mean that one person is right and the other wrong. Differences are simply that, and parents need to learn how to tolerate them rather than attempting to eradicate them. Children's "rights," their constantly changing wishes and capacities for responsibility and independence, and parental styles of discipline and limit-setting are among some of the issues that inevitably bring parental differences out in the open.

How do we typically settle our differences over raising children? The most common method is that the parent who is louder, more intimidating, or the more persistent gets his or her way. In moments when differences are most acute, it is always easier to throw up one's hands and defer to a more strident partner. But we do so with a potentially heavy price tag; loudness, intimidation, and blind persistence don't lead to the best decisions.

"It really irritates me the amount of time my son spends in front of the television watching mindless cartoons or playing video games," complains a young father. "I think my wife lets him do it so he'll be out of her hair and so she doesn't have to deal with him." The truth is that the wife does occasionally use the television as a baby-sitter, because she feels overwhelmed by the variety of activities she must somehow juggle. As she says, "The only peace and quiet I get is when Kelly is playing in his room and watching TV. I don't use that time to eat bonbons, to read—which I love—or to have nice long chats with my friends. I use it to get the things done I have to do. And that includes paying some attention to Kelly's little sister. I admit it, it's a relief sometimes when he is off in his room entertaining himself. Is that so bad?" Obviously not—it's all a matter of degree. Mothers do need time out from the intense demands children make, and television is certainly an easy solution. The issue is moderation. Fathers tend to walk in at the busiest time of day when mothers are most stressed and exhausted. Often parents complain about differences that are more apparent than real. This father needs to stop criticizing his wife for being a neglectful mother and do what he can do to alter the situation by spending more time with his son himself.

What about differences in what we see as safe for our children? Many fathers encourage independence earlier than do their wives, who are often more protective. How old should she be when she rides her bike to school? Do we let him play tackle football? What about a driver's license? How about using the family car or getting one of their own? The easier rule is to proceed at the rate of the most cautious parent because it causes him or her less anxiety. But what about the welfare of the child? The child may be better helped if the other parent comes up with some workable plan that will permit the child to move reasonably and responsibly toward greater autonomy. This will gradually reduce the more cautious parent's worry and discomfort as the child proves that new experiences can be safe and new responsibilities can be met. Such an approach requires a lot of thought and effort but is ultimately much more helpful to the child.

Taking Sides

We all intend to be loyal to the members of our family, but often we are torn and bewildered by how and to whom to show that loyalty. Louise and John have conflicts over loyalty that are acted out repeatedly with their 12-year-old son, Jason. "Every time I get upset at Jason," Louise explains, "John feels the need to step in between us. I know I lose my temper sometimes and I'm not always calm and reasonable, but I do wish he would trust me enough to let the two of us thrash out our problems without constantly playing referee. I feel John is being disloyal to me. It's as if he were treating me like one of the kids."

John doesn't feel disloyal to Louise, but he does feel a stronger sense of loyalty to his own notion of fair play and to the feelings of his son. The truth is that John does need to trust his wife's judgment more and learn to back off a bit. On the other hand, Louise needs to take responsibility for exercising a bit more control. She knows all too well that all she has to do is get into an argument with Jason and John will come running ready to spread oil on the troubled waters. John and Louise play a destructive game, and the real loser is their son, who hasn't learned he can speak up for himself rather than soliciting the sympathetic intervention of the "good" father against the "bad" mother.

Parents need to get together and decide on some rough guidelines for expressing emotion in general and angry feelings in particular. Within those guidelines, there should be fairly wide latitude in how we relate to our children, for freedom from judgment and censure is the only thing that builds trust and encourages sensitivity and discretion.

Becoming Self-Directed parents requires responding as a relatively consistent team, and that takes understanding negative themes that endlessly play themselves out and stopping them. Neither parent can selfishly believe everything should always go his or her way. Effective parenting always involves the more generous and less self-centered commitment to developing an "our way."

Getting Lost in the Children

Children absorb an incredible amount of our time and attention. When we have children, feelings of romance tend to get lost, for we must broaden our definition of love to include the family as a unit. But as much focus and energy as children realistically do take, we also need to reserve time to be together not simply as parents but as husband and wife.

Children are easy to love. But problems can arise if children are used to fill voids in the relationship or to avoid certain important conflicts. It isn't fair to children to use them as substitute love objects even if we are feeling deprived or thwarted by our partner. And it isn't fair to our partner to give all of our time and attention to the children and none to him or her. Conflict can arise if we feel shut out by our mate. Such situations are out of balance and not only cause resentment but place inappropriate pressures upon the child to do and be something only an adult can do or be.

Eva feels a vague estrangement from her husband, Lionel, and her attempts to talk to him about it always seem to dig her into a deeper hole. "I know this probably sounds stupid," she says, "but I feel jealous of Lionel's relationship with Lee, our son. I think he'd much rather be off doing something with him than with me. Lionel coaches the soccer team, they jog together after work, and they take long bike rides on the weekends. I always feel like a crazy demanding ogre when I complain, but I wish he felt the need to block out some time with me when we could just be together and talk, the way he always manages to make time for Lee. Everyone thinks Lionel is the ideal father, and I guess he is, but I feel I'm slowly losing my husband."

Lionel does need to rethink his priorities and be more generous in his time with Eva. But her complaints don't help. A better solution for Eva would be to include herself as a participant in more of their activities and to say something like the following to Lionel: "I think you're a wonderful father and I don't want you to spend less time with Lee, but I do want us to do more together. I'd like to come along on your outings with Lee, and I'd also like to set aside a couple of evenings a week for the two of us to be alone."

Too often, couples lose track of the very things they most enjoyed doing with each other, particularly when faced with the enervating demands of family life. Lest we suffer the empty-nest syndrome as our children inevitably grow up and leave us, we must not forget the importance of continuing to spend time with each other.

THE FAMILY PLAN

In order for mothers and fathers to be Self-Directed as a unit, they must take responsibility, seize the initiative—today more than ever. Yet, an evolving plan or set of guidelines about family life is conspicuously absent in most families. When we have our first child, most of us discuss what it will be like to be parents, but these talks are related, for the most part, to exploring how having children will alter the structure of our lives. We may share our anxiety about being replaced in our spouse's affections or about the rather awesome responsibility we've undertaken, but few of us put together our thoughts about what we want for our children and what we are willing to give them.

Even as our children begin to grow, most of us still don't take the time to sit down and hammer out any sort of organized plan. We spend more time watching Monday-night football, or flipping through our L. L. Bean catalogues. It's not that we don't care or aren't interested in our children's welfare, for we are. It's simply a matter of motivation. Most of us are used to responding to the demands imposed upon us but enjoy a brief moment of respite from those responsibilities. Our children don't insist that we organize our thoughts and attitudes about them, so most of us just tend to drift along, content to merely react rather than more actively shape the experience of our family.

What is helpful is the development of some sort of plan. Obviously, no two couples will have identical plans, for such plans are the expression of their individual values, thoughts, and interests, as intricate and unique as fingerprints. But a plan does have common component parts.

What We Have to Do

Caring for a child requires an immense expenditure of ongoing effort and attention to detail. Most parents are exhausted at the end of the day, and no wonder! The jobs they perform on a daily basis tax energy, patience, and resourcefulness. The following list contains some of the tasks for which parents are responsible, but this list is by no means exhaustive.

PARENTAL TASKS

CARETAKING
  1. Buy and prepare food
  2. Oversee bathing and hygiene
  3. Purchase clothing and incidentals
  4. Hire baby-sitters
  5. Care for child when sick

TRANSPORTATION
1. Drive in carpool
2. Drive or take child to friends
3. Take child to doctor and dentist

EDUCATION
1. Participate in school projects
2. Check, supervise, participate in homework
3. Teach important health and hygiene concepts
4. Attend school-related activities and conferences
5. Teach values, ethics, standards
6. Teach sex education
7. Talk about physical and emotional issues

PLAY
1. Read to child
2. Play games with child
3. Arrange for sports activities (organized and home-related)
4. Organize recreation
5. Organize birthday parties, special events

DISCIPLINE
1. Develop an evolving set of ground rules and guidelines
2. Enforce forms of discipline appropriate to age and development of the child

COMMUNICATION
1. Assist in emotional and interpersonal development

2. Translate the child's feelings into words
3. Help the child understand his or her feelings
4. Help the child both understand and deal with his or her impact upon important others

PROBLEM-SOLVING
1. Present practical and constructive ways for the child to resolve conflicts and disputes with other family members, teachers, and friends
2. Talk through the child's personal problems and develop helpful solutions, tactics, and approaches
3. Assist the child in his or her handling of such emotional dilemmas as shyness, embarrassment, anger, aggression, jealousy, hurt, rivalry, authority, limit-setting

The range of activities parents engage in with their children varies with the child's age, development, and unique circumstances. It may be useful to think through the general areas described above, adding other activities that fit more specifically into your family situation. You may be in for a bit of a surprise. We've found that when parents actually run through the list of child-related jobs they do, they are shocked at the task at hand.

In constructing the family plan, it will be helpful to take the activities listed above and individualize them to fit the unique aspects of your family.

What We Want Our Child to Be

We all have different expectations for our children, and those expectations change constantly as our children grow and develop. We need to talk about what these expectations are to be sure we are not giving the child confusing double messages and that our expectations are not unrealistic or inappropriate. Mothers and fathers certainly need not agree on all of those expectations, but there should be some understanding about what they are and how we define them. How independent do we expect our children to be? How responsible, and for what? How communicative? How obedient? How individualistic or like us? What kind of balance do we want between education, athletics, and other interests? And so on, sorting out all the feelings, concerns, and wishes.

Fathers and mothers often assume they understand each other's expectations for the child. Often this is not true. Creating a dialogue about expectations can clarify not only specific attitudes but some of the important reasons these attitudes are held. For example, a mother may want her daughter to be more independent and able to do more things alone without the father's vigilant supervision. The father may hold the same long-term goal for autonomy but not know how to deal with some of his protective feelings, even if he understands that they may be excessive. Discussing their expectations about independence, how it is defined and expressed, may reveal some specific ways they can move toward a commonly held goal.

Who Is Better at What?

After we have carefully examined the variety of expectations we have for our children, it is important to make an assessment of our basic strengths and weaknesses as parents. We each have expectations of our partner and the nature of his or her involvement in the family system. Some of these expectations may have a strong culturally conditioned basis and may or may not suit individual personalities, strengths, and interests. It works better not to try to force our partner into a predefined role simply because society has taught us that women do this or men do that. We should discuss as honestly as possible what parental tasks we do well, what ones we are interested in, and what ones are difficult for us to do. We should also rely upon our partners for feedback and observations —what strengths and weaknesses does our partner see in us? This assessment should not be a scorecard or a way of pointing out deficiencies in our mates. Rather, it is an attempt to come up with a realistic method of agreeing who can be counted on for what, based upon objectivity and inclination rather than sexual stereotypes.

Once you've looked at expectations, the tasks at hand, and your basic strengths and weaknesses, the next step is to begin some flexible assignment of responsibility. The emphasis here is on tailoring tasks to individual interests and aptitudes so that our own development evolves as well as our children's.

What We Teach Our Children

We, as parents, are the primary teachers of fundamental values to our children. We teach not only in direct instructional ways but probably even more through the living example of our behavior. One need only think of the typical small boy walking around the house with the same gait and body movements as his father to realize how strongly our children look to us as models. We all teach our children what is important and what works, but many of us do this unconsciously. If our children overhear us telling small lies, they will come to believe such lying is acceptable.

We teach our children through the example of what we do and how we behave, not by what intentions we may have or by the words we use. Our words and lists of shoulds carry no weight at all if they are contradicted by our actions. "Do as I say, not as I do" is not simply a bankrupt model for values teaching, it breeds an active disrespect for the parent and washes away the good along with the bad.

Laurie, 8 years old, was describing the confusion she feels about her parents. "My dad really gets mad at me if I ever talk back to my mother, but he yells and screams at her a lot, and I even hear him call her stupid. And my mom tells me I should respect my dad, but I don't think she does, 'cause she makes these weird faces at him behind his back when she's mad." Laurie is learning about respect not from her parents' words but from their emotionally charged disrespectful actions toward each other. What is sad is that they believe they are teaching Laurie "all the right things" and will be shocked when she reaches adolescence and the impact of their true lessons emerges.

If we gossip and backbite within earshot of our children, they will learn that gossiping and backbiting are acceptable. Saying "You didn't hear that!" or "Don't you ever tell Grandma what I said" doesn't negate the message. The child learns that hostility, disloyalty, and cruelty are acceptable as long as they are expressed indirectly or furtively. If we want to teach honesty and forthrightness we have to be honest and forthright.

Even simple dignity and entitlement need to be taught through our actions. Suzie has just reached adolescence and is struggling with feelings of self-worth. "My mom tells me I should learn how to stick up for myself," she says, "but I see what she puts up with from my dad and she never opens her mouth. She blows up at me and my little brother, but I've never seen her call my dad on some of the things he does." If we give and demand sensitivity and dignity, that will be taught. If we don't, lessons such as Suzie is learning will be the legacy.

Values differ across a broad spectrum, reflecting wide individual differences. The specifics of one's values and approaches toward life are important. But even more important is taking the time to actually think them through and put them into words with our partner. This requires taking stock of how we really behave, not just how we would like to behave. For many of us, this is a first-time experience, but the energy expended is well worth it to help articulate and clarify not only the values you *are* teaching your children but the ones you would *like* to be teaching them.

Dealing with Conflict

Conflict normally exists in all of our families. It is a natural by-product of our differences as human beings and the stresses of day-to-day living. Sometimes we may want to give up and walk away or just plain explode. More constructive, however, is developing some less helpless method for dealing with conflict. Again, there are wide individual differences, and therefore widely different methods of resolving problems, disagreements, and disputes. Whether we agree to work things out in a weekly family meeting and discussion or in some other way, what is critical is that we agree to do *something*— that we develop a plan that everyone knows about and can count on.

In a family, conflict centers around the feelings and reactions family members have about their various interconnected relationships and, more specifically, around issues of children's independence and responsibility. The reason conflict is such a thorny problem is that our feelings don't change simply because someone else feels differently. For that reason, most family conflict is resolved by power, not rationality. If "might makes right," "right" is held firmly by the dominant parent. However, resolution through power is often rigid and poorly informed and becomes progressively less effective as the children get older. "It's right because I say so!" works for a 4-year-old but may not work for a 14-year-old.

Another all too common approach is conflict resolution through passivity. While ignoring certain issues certainly is easier and less emotionally draining than confronting them, it is also fundamentally irresponsible and results in a kind of family anarchy and haphazard child development.

What then is the answer? Parents are bosses, right? You can't run a family like a democracy, right? There has to be a leader, someone who is ultimately responsible for coming up with a decision, right? Yes to all of the above, but that doesn't mean that some uninformed self-appointed dictator gets to call all the shots. Positive conflict resolution involves being informed, understanding how children change as they grow, and keeping abreast of what is appropriate given their age and maturity. Constructive conflict resolution requires consistency and parents working as a team. And it requires listening and talking to the child with openness and a flexible attitude when he or she mounts a convincing argument.

"We set aside time every Sunday night for a gripe session," recalls Craig, a 16-year-old boy. "In the beginning, it could get pretty hot and heavy, but now half the time nobody has anything big to say, so we all just talk. I used to feel like I lived in Russia, like I was their slave or something, but now it's different. I still don't get my way all that often, but I feel like they listen to me, and even when they say no it makes more sense, because we've talked about it." Gripe sessions, family meetings, bedtime "conversations," whatever you call it—what works is some regular forum for discussion where feelings, wishes, and concerns can all be aired. Sure, someone still needs to be the final decision-maker, and no, not everyone's desires will magically be satisfied. But the family will feel that decisions have been made in a more responsible, informed, and supportive way. And that's as good as any of us can do.

What We Hope for the Future

"For me, growing up felt like I was totally alone and on my own. Enough time passed, and we all left home, turning out any which way," Pamela recounts. "I don't want it to be that way with my kids. Dale and I really make an effort to know and understand our children as individuals. We want them to be able to talk to us without feeling embarrassed or intimidated—and I don't mean like pals because I don't believe a parent should be like a best friend. Dale and I have made a decision that family comes first—the time and money that's left over we use for our personal enjoyment. We take family vacations and try and do regular outings with everybody included. Dale and I have worked out some pretty specific rules and guidelines, I guess partly because I hated the lack of structure and stability I had when I was a kid. We like to talk about the kids—things we'd like to do with them, trying to keep one step ahead of them, which is no easy trick—and I must admit, we also enjoy talking about and planning for the future, what we might like to do after the kids are grown and gone."

Arthur and Nadine have a different vision for their family. Arthur says, "We've seen a lot of couples pay all kinds of attention to their children and drift away from each other in the process. I think we both feel that we'll be better parents to Bret if we feel good about each other—that's real important. Nadine and I both came from pretty sheltered families where doing anything our parents didn't do was seen as bad. We're trying to be different and give Bret more latitude and freedom. There obviously have to be limits, but we try to keep them reasonable so he has some room to stretch himself. We're also a pretty emotional family, and there aren't any hard-and-fast rules about language or expressing feelings. We see our primary job as making sure Bret grows up strong and independent and really knowing who he is."

As parents, exactly what you stand for isn't so important, but that you stand for something that reflects thought and planning is important. We all have ideas and dreams about our families—how we would like to live, what we would like to do, and how we would like to be with each other. But for many of us, this vision is articulated not at all, or only in a fragmentary way. Developing a plan for the structure and direction of the family can be not only useful but fun. It allows us to dream together, which creates the truly special feelings of closeness and bonding. If this is the family we've created, how can we make it the most meaningful, supportive, and warm experience possible? The discussion and definition of a family vision is an evolutionary process and one that should always be undergoing fine-tuning to keep up with change and the passage of time. The whole notion of a family plan is continuity—there is little point in talking about issues a couple of times and then forgetting them. Continuity means keeping the plan alive and relating positively and realistically to the ongoing events and changes that we go through in our lives.

The family plan is a conscious and personally responsible commitment we make to our family. It actually takes quite a bit of thought, soul-searching, and energy. But those who take on the challenge of the task will be richly rewarded. It should not be surprising that family, the one facet of marriage that requires the setting aside of selfish concerns, is the area that yields the most gratification.

A New Way of Being Together

*W*e began this book with the observation that in spite of the concerns lingering in the minds of most couples, wives and husbands are more committed to each other than ever before. In a sense, what we have been describing is the heart of what that commitment must be: to discriminate, honestly and even painfully, between the idealized myths we have learned and the real potential of marriage.

Marriages that will thrive in the next decade will be those that are Self-Directed, those in which each person takes on the personal responsibility for making love happen rather than passively waiting or looking to his or her spouse to create a sense of aliveness. We believe that husbands and wives will finally discover a perspective that enables them to take actions on their own that will ultimately gain them more fulfillment than a demanding and implicitly unaccepting Other-Directed marriage. The 1990s marriage will be guided by a set of attitudes that will create even greater intimacy than we could have imagined. Let us examine these new rules that are just now evolving.

Husbands and Wives Will Become Self-Directed

Confronting a new perspective is a daunting task, regardless of the eventual rewards that may follow. As psychologists working with couples, and as husbands ourselves, we know that simplistic explanations and solutions for marital unrest may seem reassuring even though they are ultimately frustrating because they simply don't work. We also know that looking at our marriages from a new and different angle, shifting from subjectivity to objectivity, is much more difficult than our words may imply. Breaking old patterns is never easy. We are so conditioned to ascribe blame, to look for causality someplace outside of ourselves, that grappling with personal responsibility makes us feel somewhat helpless at first. We have become so accustomed to believing our mate is supposed to make us happy, supposed to provide solutions to old painful dilemmas, and supposed to change in ways that match our evolving emotional needs that it is hard to believe otherwise. If we can't get our mate to change, what hope is there?

Yet, if our message has been presented clearly, we are saying it is at that very moment of apparent powerlessness that change first begins. The fact is, we are powerless when it comes to changing our partners, but we are powerful when we look to ourselves as the source of new and more constructive experiences. It is only then that we can truly shape our marital destiny.

Letting Go Will Be Liberating

The thematic thread running throughout our observations is one of letting go, whether it is having the courage to disconnect momentarily from the tenacious dependency we all have on our spouses, or letting go of cherished fantasies and expectations that are in fact impossible to realize in any relationship. Our promise, however, is that releasing oneself and one's mate from such expectations leads to greater love.

Couples who will courageously examine their own hidden agendas—those complex clusters of expectations, myths, and false assumptions—and take responsibility for having imposed them, often blindly and haphazardly, on the delicate marriage structure will discover the strength that comes from standing back and grappling with a fresh perspective. These couples will come to realize that disillusionment is not an indictment of them personally, their spouse, or even the quality of their marriage, but a natural process that follows our having been taught to be Other-Directed in our relationships. They will come to realize the paradox of communication—that instead of simply letting our mate know who we are, we are too often letting our mate know what he or she is not. These couples will realize that fearing instability only leads to a stagnation that is, at best, benign. They will realize that trust is not communicated by words, but by actions based on unselfish loving. And finally, these couples will begin to see that when marriage stops being adversarial, it becomes a shared adventure with both anxious and joyous times.

Acceptance Will Be the Catalyst for Change

In the 1990s, couples will finally realize that the only way to make each other secure enough to risk new ways of behaving and to give more freely is to accept each other. Couples will understand that acceptance is not resignation—rather it is a perception of each other that evolves out of love rather than criticism and blame. Moreover, the person who does the accepting will feel better about himself or herself, because we all feel good when we are secure enough to accept who our mate really is. Husbands and wives will discover that acceptance is not simply an endorsement of the status quo, but rather an acknowledgment that who you're married to is still someone you continue to love despite his or her imperfections and difficulties in accommodating your wishes. The reward for the acceptor will be to discover that acceptance creates security and then change in the other person.

Disenchantment Will Become a Challenge Rather Than an Indictment

So many marriages today are beset by secret pessimism, secret suspicion that the love which originally led to a wish to marry is no longer alive, no longer present in daily exchanges between husband and wife. That pessimism is understandable but wrong. It is based on the subtle estrangements that seem evident at the time, not on what is actually possible in any marriage. Letting go of impossible expectations detoxifies a relationship, relieving marital partners from the burden of blame and resentment. This emotional release allows dormant love to become revived. Indeed, it is only at this time in the life of a marriage that a genuine marital pact can evolve.

In the next decade, couples will come to regard disappointments and disillusionment as a natural part of marriage, not necessarily as indications of a "bad" relationship. They will know that even the best of marriages have bad times, and that feelings of disenchantment are simply a clear signal for both parties to take a fresh look at what is not happening between them.

Couples Will Create a Marriage Pact

What does a marriage mean? What kind of marriage do we have? What kind do we want? When we first marry, most of us passively accept a conventional view of marriage. Coming to grips with who we are together, our unique gifts as well as our unique shortcomings, is the task of every marriage. Overcoming the subtle disenchantments that occur in any marriage is the process leading to a pact that is truly of our own design. As our marriage evolves over the years, it is this pact that provides the lifeline of love and a sense of permanence even while change is always taking place.

Future marriages will be based on assumptions and shared visions that will be more explicit and more conscious.

Friendship Will Be the Cornerstone

Couples will finally integrate the social upheavals of the last few decades. Differences will be cherished and viewed as stimulating rather than threatening. Friendship, which has always been the spine of the best marriages, will be actively fostered. Husbands and wives will finally have learned that friendship and sexual attraction are not incompatible.

Our concluding message is to trust your basic

resilience, trust the love that brought you and your mate together, and finally trust your own courage to confront the realities of marriage today. If you do, you will discover the security, pleasure, excitement, and inevitability of the love that will be yours in return.

Patterns of Approval

ACCEPTING ONE'S MATE: A QUIZ

1. I've learned how to forgive and let go of
   the little everyday annoyances my mate
   causes me.
   T _____ F _____

2. I often feel angry at my mate.
   T _____ F _____

3. I don't particularly enjoy doing many of
   the things my mate likes to do, and I
   don't do things that are of no interest
   to me.
   T _____ F _____

4. I can remember my parents fighting and
   being angry a lot.
   T _____ F _____

5. One or both of my parents abused alcohol or drugs.
   T _____ F _____

6. I was abused as a child.
   T _____ F _____

7. The treatment I receive from my mate is consistent with my expectations of marriage.
   T _____ F _____

8. I frequently try to make my mate feel guilty.
   T _____ F _____

9. I don't expect to be the center of my mate's life.
   T _____ F _____

10. When I give I expect to get back in like fashion.
    T _____ F _____

11. I can be nurturing or protective with my mate without necessarily feeling parental.
    T _____ F _____

12. I see my mate as an equal.
    T _____ F _____

13. I'm not aware of setting up double standards in my marriage.
    T _____ F _____

14. I believe that I really understand my
    mate.
    T _____ F _____

15. I must admit I am afraid and cautious
    with my mate.
    T _____ F _____

16. I think I've given up most of my wishful
    illusions about my mate and enjoy my
    mate anyway.
    T _____ F _____

17. I've never really had or been able to
    maintain a strong platonic friendship
    with someone of the opposite sex.
    T _____ F _____

18. There's a definite right way and a wrong
    way of doing things.
    T _____ F _____

19. I've been told that I'm critical and
    somewhat of a perfectionist.
    T _____ F _____

20. I like to share confidences with my mate
    and feel safe doing so.
    T _____ F _____

21. My mate feels loved and secure with me.
    T _____ F _____

22. My mate seems to confide more in friends than in me.

    T _____ F _____

23. I'm basically approving and supportive of my mate's relationships with friends.

    T _____ F _____

24. I often wish that my mate looked different.

    T _____ F _____

25. Sometimes I feel we are too different to be a good match.

    T _____ F _____

26. I must admit I hold many secret resentments toward my mate.

    T _____ F _____

27. The way we divide up responsibilities feels comfortable to me.

    T _____ F _____

28. I like the way my mate and I are sexually.

    T _____ F _____

29. I really enjoy it when my mate is happy even if those good feelings have nothing to do with me.

    T _____ F _____

30. My mate's need for privacy and time alone bothers me.

    T _____ F _____

SCORING

Score one point for any of the following marked T: 1, 7, 9, 11, 12, 13, 14, 16, 20, 21, 23, 27, 28, 29.

Score one point for any of the following marked F: 2, 3, 4, 5, 6, 8, 10, 15, 17, 18, 19, 22, 24, 25, 26, 30.

Add up your score.

INTERPRETATION

26—30: You truly seem to enjoy and accept your mate. Whatever flaws or imperfections you may see tend to become more background than foreground. Basically, you provide an emotional environment that is safe and nurturing and one that allows for considerable growth and individual expression. Your mate is indeed fortunate to have you as a marriage partner.

21—25: You believe yourself to be quite accepting of your mate, although you may be bothered by certain feelings of distrust or resentment. Such feelings may cause you to be somewhat self-protective at times, resulting in your mate's feeling cautious with you. It may be important to explore the possibility of a slight tendency to be a perfectionist and to assume that your way is always the more correct way.

16—20: It is likely that you may be more concerned with receiving understanding from your mate than you are with giving acceptance. While you are probably equally hard upon yourself, your mate is likely to feel criticized and deficient at times. Control may be an important issue for you to explore. Forgiving your own imperfections may also enable your mate to be more spontaneous and comfortable.

15 or less: It is likely that you struggle with being overly critical, controlling, and distrustful. It is equally likely that your mate feels unaccepted in certain fundamental ways and inadequate in your eyes. While much of your behavior may be self-protective and related to avoiding hurt and disappointment, your mate may not recognize this fact and simply feel lacking and unloved.

HOW ACCEPTED BY MY HUSBAND DO I FEEL?

1. Sometimes I get the feeling that I'm not enough for my husband.
   T _____ F _____

2. My husband encourages and supports me and is comfortable with my strength, success, and intelligence.
   T _____ F _____

3. My husband sometimes seems to ridicule or belittle my achievements.
   T _____ F _____

4. My husband would prefer me to be somewhat dependent on him.

T _____ F _____

5. When I try to diet, exercise, or better my appearance, I get the feeling that my husband is secretly sabotaging my efforts.

T _____ F _____

6. My husband seems angry at me a lot.

T _____ F _____

7. My husband feels comfortable when I'm outgoing and assertive.

T _____ F _____

8. My husband enjoys it when I initiate sexual contact.

T _____ F _____

9. My husband is satisfied with our sex life.

T _____ F _____

10. My husband likes the way I look.

T _____ F _____

11. I feel "heard" and understood by my husband.

T _____ F _____

12. My husband thinks my wish for friendship

is simply a disguised way of asking for romance and intimacy.

T _____   F _____

13. My husband doesn't always "have to be right."

T _____   F _____

14. I feel put on a pedestal by my husband.

T _____   F _____

15. My husband approaches me as an equal.

T _____   F _____

16. My husband clearly sees the "real me" and likes it.

T _____   F _____

17. My husband would describe me to others not only as a wife but as a close friend.

T _____   F _____

18. From my husband's point of view, I'm "too romantic" at times.

T _____   F _____

19. My husband enjoys doing what I'm particularly interested in at times.

T _____   F _____

20. My husband can sometimes be cruel or humiliating in his comments to me.

T _____   F _____

21. Often I feel a vague sense of guilt or inadequacy as a wife.
    T _____ F _____

22. My husband brings up my flaws or shortcomings around other people.
    T _____ F _____

23. My husband has a deep sense of trust in me.
    T _____ F _____

24. My husband can become very jealous even when there is no basis for him to feel that way.
    T _____ F _____

25. My husband would not be threatened by my having a close platonic relationship with a male friend.
    T _____ F _____

26. I often feel that my husband is critical of my women friends.
    T _____ F _____

27. My husband respects my needs for contact and conversation as well as my needs for privacy and time alone.
    T _____ F _____

28. My husband allows me to be different from him without making me feel guilty.
    T _____ F _____

29. My husband is good about accepting our differences.

   T _____ F _____

30. I often feel embarrassed when my husband sees me without my clothes.

   T _____ F _____

SCORING

Add one point for each of the following marked T: 2, 7, 8, 9, 10, 11, 13, 15, 16, 17, 19, 23, 25, 27, 28, 29.

Add one point for each of the following marked F: 1, 3, 4, 5, 6, 12, 14, 18, 20, 21, 22, 24, 26, 30.

Add up your score.

INTERPRETATION

26—30: In most areas you feel comfortable, loved, and accepted by your husband. He is not threatened by your individuality, strength, or personal freedom. You are fortunate to have found someone who so generously gives the uncritical love we all so desire.

21—25: In an overall way, you feel understood and accepted by your husband. However, there are certain critical areas in which you feel his approval is withheld. It may be helpful for you to bring up some of your concerns. They may turn out to be more fears or inaccurate assumptions on your part than facts, for it is clear that in general he has strong positive feelings for you.

16—20: You have some serious concerns and doubts about being lovable in your husband's eyes. Too often you feel criticized, distrusted, and controlled, and too often you believe you are unloved and misunderstood. Such levels of distrust and rigid judgment leave permanent marks. Don't wait too long to address these important issues directly and honestly with your husband.

15 or below: You feel misunderstood and unappreciated pretty much across the board. Love cannot be sustained for long with this level of harsh, ungiving judgment.

HOW ACCEPTED BY MY WIFE DO I FEEL?

1. My wife thinks I am a workaholic and don't give our relationship the time and attention it deserves.
   T _____ F _____

2. My wife is resentful of the time I spend with my men friends or watching sports on TV.
   T _____ F _____

3. Often my wife seems angry at me.
   T _____ F _____

4. My wife can handle my being playful or boyish sometimes.
   T _____ F _____

5. My wife thinks we have a good balance of shared responsibilities.
   T _____ F _____

6. If I feel vulnerable or insecure around my wife, she is not turned off or upset.
   T _____ F _____

7. My wife sees me as her friend as well as her mate.
   T _____ F _____

8. There are few secrets about me my wife doesn't know and accept.
   T _____ F _____

9. My wife thinks I am (or would be) a good father.
   T _____ F _____

10. My wife frequently points out my shortcomings.
    T _____ F _____

11. I feel my wife has expectations of me I can't meet.

    T _____ F _____

12. My wife would like me to be more romantic with her.

    T _____ F _____

13. Basically, I feel understood by my wife.

    T _____ F _____

14. Frequently, my wife seems overly critical and judgmental of me.

    T _____ F _____

15. My wife is uncomfortable with the thought of my ever being dependent upon her.

    T _____ F _____

16. My wife can be nurturing with me without feeling as though she is my mother.

    T _____ F _____

17. My wife likes my appearance.

    T _____ F _____

18. My wife is satisfied with our sex life.

    T _____ F _____

19. My wife doesn't think I'm emotionally expressive enough.

    T _____ F _____

20. My wife approaches me as an equal.
    T _____ F _____

21. My wife has strong needs for control in
    the relationship.
    T _____ F _____

22. My wife really knows who I am and likes
    me.
    T _____ F _____

23. My wife enjoys occasionally doing things
    that are of particular interest to me.
    T _____ F _____

24. My wife can be hostile to me or humiliate
    me around other people.
    T _____ F _____

25. My wife has a deep sense of trust in me.
    T _____ F _____

26. My wife likes and enjoys my men friends.
    T _____ F _____

27. My wife can be excessively jealous and
    possessive even when there is no reason
    to be.
    T _____ F _____

28. My wife accepts our differences without
    making me feel guilty about them.
    T _____ F _____

29. My wife would not be threatened by my having a close nonromantic relationship with a woman.

T _____   F _____

30. My wife gets along well with my parents.

T _____   F _____

SCORING

Add one point for each of the following marked T: 4, 5, 6, 7, 8, 9, 13, 16, 17, 18, 20, 22, 23, 25, 26, 28, 29, 30.

Add one point for each of the following marked F: 1, 2, 3, 10, 11, 12, 14, 15, 19, 21, 24, 27.

Add up your score.

INTERPRETATION

26—30: You are indeed a lucky man—your wife loves and accepts you despite your flaws and shortcomings. Such generous and unconditional love should not go unnoticed or unacknowledged. Tell her how much you appreciate her support and friendship.

21—25: Generally, you feel a broad level of caring acceptance from your wife, although you are aware that there are certain things she reacts to negatively. Be pleased that so many aspects of your personality are accepted. What's not should not become the fuel for endless discussions and negotiation.

16—20: You feel distrusted and criticized about much of your conduct in the marriage. Such important levels of disregard have a cumulative effect and must be addressed. Otherwise, you will be left feeling chronically inadequate. But, before you see this as all her problem, make sure you clearly examine your own behavior and be certain you are proud of it.

15 and below: You feel under siege in many areas of your relationship. Such a serious lack of acceptance must be addressed directly with your wife, for you feel neither loved nor understood.